重庆第二师范学院重大委托课题“核心素养背景下儿童‘融思促学’特色资源开发”（批准号：2017XJZDWT03）
重庆市社科规划项目“儿童英语阅读能力与思维技能双发展实验研究”（批准号：2019YBJJ107）
重庆第二师范学院科研平台“儿童外语教育协同创新中心”（编号：201605）阶段研究成果

小学英语融思促学活动设计与应用

Xiaoxue Yingyu Rongsi Cuxue Huodong Sheji Yu Yingyong

周利君　向小婷　邹　娟　编著

重庆大学出版社

图书在版编目（CIP）数据

小学英语融思促学活动设计与应用 / 周利君，向小婷，邹娟编著. -- 重庆：重庆大学出版社，2020.11

ISBN 978-7-5689-2500-6

Ⅰ. ①小… Ⅱ. ①周… ②向… ③邹… Ⅲ. ①英语课—教学设计—小学 Ⅳ. ① G623.312

中国版本图书馆CIP数据核字（2020）第232868号

小学英语融思促学活动设计与应用

周利君 向小婷 邹 娟 编著

责任编辑：陈 亮 版式设计：周永梅 陈 亮

责任校对：王 倩 责任印制：赵 晟

*

重庆大学出版社出版发行

出版人：饶帮华

社址：重庆市沙坪坝区大学城西路21号

邮编：401331

电话：（023）88617190 88617185（中小学）

传真：（023）88617186 88617166

网址：http://www.cqup.com.cn

邮箱：fxk@cqup.com.cn（营销中心）

全国新华书店经销

重庆升光电力印务有限公司印刷

*

开本：787mm×1092mm 1/16 印张：12.75 字数：374千

2020年12月第1版 2020年12月第1次印刷

ISBN 978-7-5689-2500-6 定价：59.00元

XUYAN
序言

记得2011年，我在北京给小学教师做讲座的时候提到如何通过英语教学培养学生的思维能力，很多教师还不是很理解。当时主流的观点是：外语教学首先要培养学生的语言能力，要积累一定的语言技能、词汇、语法、句型等，然后才能谈别的方面。如果学生没有这些语言的基础，就无法培养思维能力。

实际上，学生从学习语言的第一天开始，就涉及思维能力的培养。我访问过好几所美国的小学，儿童在学前就已经开始进行思维能力的培养，比如区分“事实与观点（facts or opinions）”。几乎每所学校，都把要培养的几种思维能力，贴在教室墙上，这给我留下了深刻印象。

我想，初学英语的学生，虽然开始接触的语言很少，但是完全可以培养思维能力。举个例子：苹果有营养是“事实”，某种苹果最好吃是“观点”。只是我们的教师需要知道，应该培养哪些方面的思维能力，比如说：原因和结果、分类、推断、归纳等；更为重要的是：教师们还需要知道，如何培养这些思维能力，什么任务活动有助于培养这些思维能力，可以借助什么工具等。

最近几年，随着国家课程标准的修订，关于培养学生核心素养的要求已成为教师们讨论的热点话题，特别是品格培养和思维培养这两个方面。教师们感到，基础教育的目标应该是人的全面发展，必须培养学生的思维能力和品格。但是，究竟如何做，对思维的分类、内涵、范畴等，现在还缺乏明确的定义，更缺乏非常清晰的指导。到底培养学生哪些方面的思维能力，通过什么样的活动能培养这些思维能力，教师们缺乏现成的、方便实用的资料。我很高兴看到，重庆第二师范学院周利君老师带领的团队设计出这样一套适合小学高段学生和教师使用的小学英语融思促学活动资源。这真是及时雨！

这套活动资源的学生版可用于学生学习、亲子学习；教师版可用于教学的补充资源、校本课程，也可作为提高教师专业知识与能力的学习材料。所以在这里，一方面，我要对周老师及其团队表示衷心的祝贺；另一方面，也希望有更多的中小学英语教师能积极应用这套活动资源，将发展学生的思维能力、良好品格和行为习惯与培养英语运用能力结合起来。我也希望有更多的教师，能受到这套活动资源的启发，在自己的学校开展各种创造性的活动，共同铺建英语教育的新路。

龚亚夫

2020年7月4日

QIANYAN

前言

语言是思维的外壳，思维是语言的内在。核心素养背景下，学习者语言能力与思维能力同步发展成为广大一线教师开展英语教学改革与科学研究的重要课题之一。

布鲁姆等1956年提出的教育目标分类体系被国际教育界广泛采用。随着分类体系研究的发展，安德森等汇集认知心理学、课程研究、教育研究和语言测试等方面的研究成果，发布了更符合21世纪教育教学改革发展的教育目标分类体系修订版，主要包括认知过程和知识两个维度。其中，认知过程维度包括六大类别，每一类别下面又包含若干子类别的思维技能，形成由易到难、由简单到复杂的目标层次结构。相对于思维能力，思维技能理解难度系数低，以特定的思维理论框架作为英语教学的依托、涵盖不同层级思维技能的训练，在教学中具有更强的实操性。融入式思维教学将思维训练贯穿于学科日常教学中，与学科教学相辅相成。

2015年以来，重庆第二师范学院外国语言文学学院通过巴渝海外引智计划引进英国纽卡斯尔大学林梅博士和汉纳肯博士，联合开展“外语教育融思促学教研团队”（以下简称“团队”）建设，对合作基地小学优秀师资和院内英语师范专业优秀学子进行培养。在这个过程中，团队多次深入一线小学英语课堂教学观摩，发现小学英语教学多重语言知识技能，轻思维训练，其主要原因在于思维理论框架复杂且较抽象，缺乏教材配套思维训练资源。自

2018年开始，团队积极致力于外语教育融思促学资源开发。2018年年底，团队选送第一批完成的融思促学活动参加国家未来学校博览会，受到来自市内外参会一线教师的肯定与欢迎。团队大受鼓舞，结合在合作基地学校开展的融思促学实验研究开发了小学英语融思促学活动，供小学高段学生和教师使用。

本套活动资源教师版和学生版与以人教版为代表的现行小学英语教材（五年级）单元话题配套，从课标中各话题下语言知识和语言技能学习要求出发，提供语言知识学习和语言技能训练的活动。单元编写体例采用Top-down的语言学习理念，从语言技能到语言知识，整体特点鲜明，具体如下：

思维技能融入的显性化。显性化途径多元，一是在学生版和教师版的活动步骤中凸显思维技能的动词表达并不断重复，有助于师生理解和记忆。二是在教师版活动过程说明之后采用思维试纸，将活动步骤与对应的思维层级相匹配，有利于教师明确所设计活动的认知复杂度，并检查单元活动设计的思维层级的多样性。三是在活动步骤旁运用提示贴纸，凸显思维工具和策略的使用说明，促使教师有意识地引导学生借助思维工具和策略强化思维训练。

思维技能融入的具体化。针对一线教师在英语教学中融入思维训练太过抽象，不知道如何在课堂中实现这一问题，活动设计教师版从一线教师角度，模拟教案形式，对教学目标设定和教学活动步骤、教学建议等进行了具体说明，帮助教师快速进入融入式教学实践。部分活动步骤说明还提供了多种方案和实施建议，给予教师空间根据自身课堂情况进行筛选和调整。

思维技能融入的全面性。思维训练方面，依据修订版的布鲁姆教育目标分类框架的认知维度，覆盖低阶思维技能和高阶思维技能。结合各单元主题情境，教学活动设计兼顾基础思维技能活动和复杂思维过程任务，关注单个技能和复杂思维的同步训练。语言教学方面，每个单元采用从整体到局部的教学思路，从听、说、读、写等语言技能入手，落实到词汇、语法等语言知识的学习，满足不同的语言教学需求。

本套活动资源是重庆第二师范学院重大委托课题“核心素养背景下儿童‘融思促学’特色资源开发”（批准号：2017XJZDWT03）、重庆市社科规划项目“儿童英语阅读能力与思维技能双发展实验研究”（批准号：2019YBJJ107）、重庆第二师范学院科研平台“儿童外语教育协同创新中心”（编号：201605）阶段研究成果，由课题负责人周利君组织设计、主持编写、审校定稿。其中5A部分由邹娟、周利君编写完成，5B部分由向小婷、周利君和陈慧贤编写完成。贺倩彧、孙亮参与统稿，部分活动由单芳、邬若环在合作基地小学进行了课堂实践后提出修订建议。本套活动资源编写过程中，得到了重庆第二师范学院外国语言文学学院领导和同事、巴渝海外引智专家、基地学校领导和同行的大力支持，在此表示衷心感谢。

由于课题组成员水平有限，难免有错漏之处，敬请各位专家和同行批评指正。

周利君

2020年7月

Contents

目 录

5A

5B

5A

Unit 1 What's He Like?

单元导览

单元话题: 人物特征
素材来源: PEP 5A Unit 1 What's He Like?
教学时长: 3 hrs
教学目标:

By the end of the lessons, students will be able to

语言目标:

1. **understand**, say and **recognize** the words describing people's features (old, young, funny, friendly, strict, helpful and kind) in English;

2. **understand** conversations in the textbook and **describe** the features of people they are familiar with by **using** the target vocabulary and some other words learned previously (short, tall, strong, thin, etc.);

3. **comprehend** the meaning of the email, **analyze** the main content and structure, and **apply** the knowledge and language in the text to writing about the robot designed by themselves;

4. **explain** reasons for their favorite teachers by **using** sentence pattern: My favorite teacher is... because he / she is...

非语言目标:

1. work in groups to **classify** people based on their features;

2. appreciate the good qualities in people;

3. strengthen higher order thinking skills: **analyzing**, **evaluating** and **creating**;

4. **design** a robot with creative thinking and **judge** with critical thinking.

融思设计

Part One Listening and Speaking

教学素材: Part B Let's Talk

教学步骤:

Step 1 Listening Comprehension

1. Listen and **tick** which teacher they are talking about.

   A. Ms. Wang. B. Mr. Li.

2. Listen again and **fill in** the blanks with words to describe what the teacher is like.

________ is ____________ and sometimes ____________.

Step 2 Preparation before Speaking

1. We have 3 new teachers. Choose proper word(s) from the Word Box and put down the letters to **match** the pictures.

Word Box

A. old	B. young	C. strict	D. funny	E. hard-working
F. kind	G. clever	H. shy	I. polite	J. tall

____

____

____

2. Read the introductions below about the 3 teachers and **find out** the similarities (相同点) and differences (不同点) between the words you choose and the words in the introductions.

1. Mr. Zhang is a young man. He is tall and thin. He looks strict but he is funny.
2. Miss Li is a young lady. She is short and thin. She is shy but she is kind.
3. Ms. Chen is an elderly lady. She is kind and hard-working.

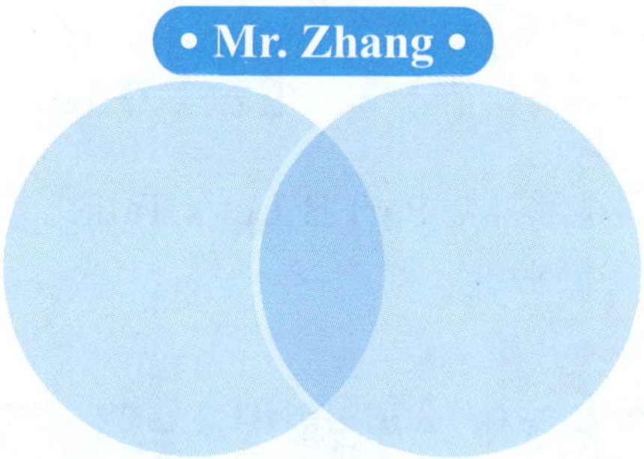

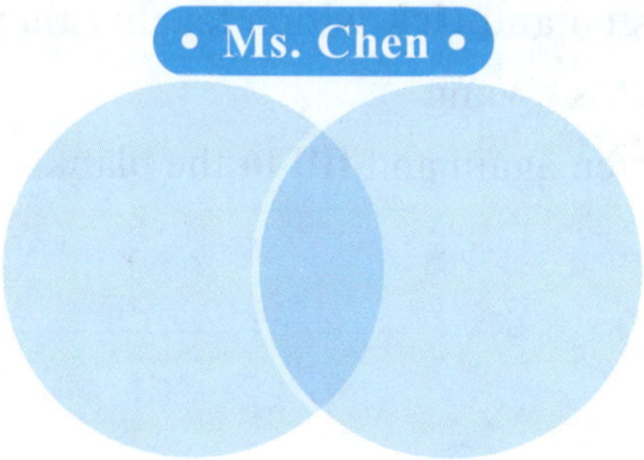

Step 3 Speaking and Sharing

1. Discuss and **make** a list of the features of your favorite teacher.

My favorite teacher is ________.
She / He is...

→ kind
...

2. **Make** a profile (简单描述) for an ideal English teacher.

Name:
Gender:
Age:
Height:
Subject:
Personality:

3. **Introduce** the teacher you create to the class.

An ideal English teacher should be / have ____________.

Word Box

pretty / beautiful	slim
patient	loving
friendly	warm-hearted
helpful	sympathetic
competent	knowledgeable

教学时长: 1.5 hrs

教学建议:

1. 听力理解环节。

(1)学生听录音，根据描述选出录音中谈论的教师。

Ms. Wang

(2)教师再次播放录音，提醒学生关注描写人物的形容词。学生听录音，完成句子填空。

Ms. Wang is kind and sometimes strict.

2. 表达准备环节。

教师引导学生观察三名新教师的照片，学生根据图片人物形象推测，从词库中选出相匹配的形容词并将字母写在横线上。教师邀请一名学生分享其做选择的依据，并询问其他同学是否赞同。教师公布三名新教师个人简介，引导学生思考并总结外貌和性格特征的关系。

Mr. Zhang is a young man. He is tall and thin. He looks strict but he is funny.

Miss Li is a young lady. She is short and thin. She is shy but she is kind.

Ms. Chen is an elderly lady. She is kind and hard-working.

3. 表达与分享环节。

(1)教师将学生分为四人一组，要求学生讨论并列举理想的英语教师的外貌和性格特点。

(2)学生小组合作，根据列举出的外貌和性格特征创造理想的英语教师形象，并为其创作个人档案。

(3)教师邀请各小组分享自己创造的理想的英语教师形象和个人档案，并引导全班同学投票选出三个最佳的教师形象。

思维试纸:

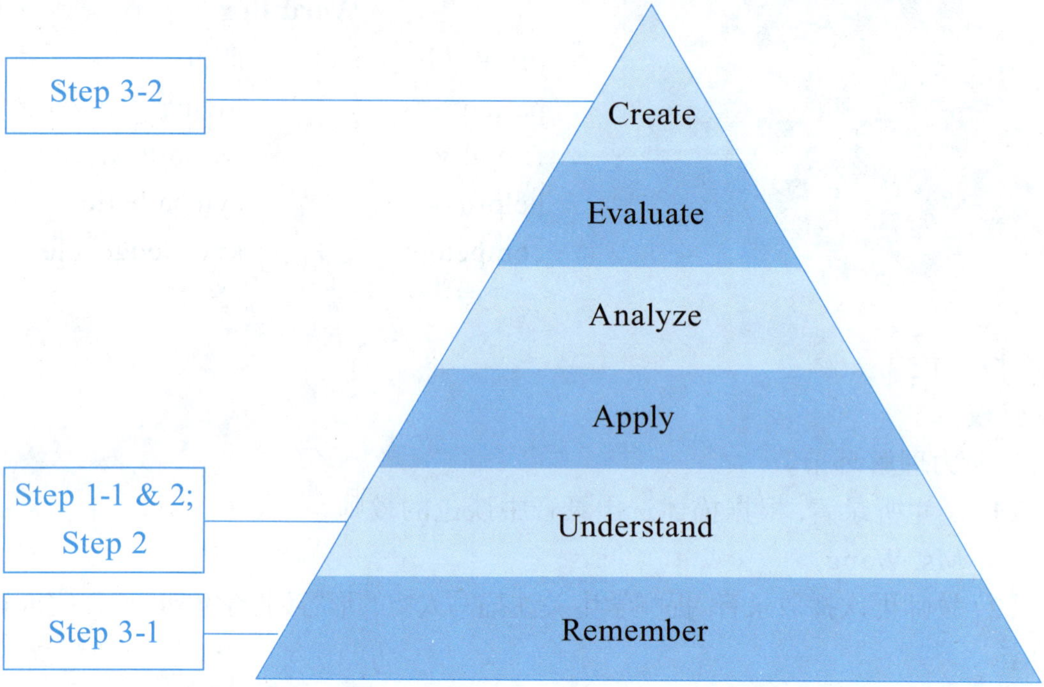

备注:“思维试纸”将各教学活动中加粗的动词(思维技能)与思维层级匹配,使教学过程中的思维技能训练显性化。5A余下各单元的“思维试纸”不再一一备注。

Part Two　Reading and Writing

教学素材: Part B Read and Write

教学步骤:

Step 1　Learning before Reading

Brainstorm: What a robot is like in a bubble map.

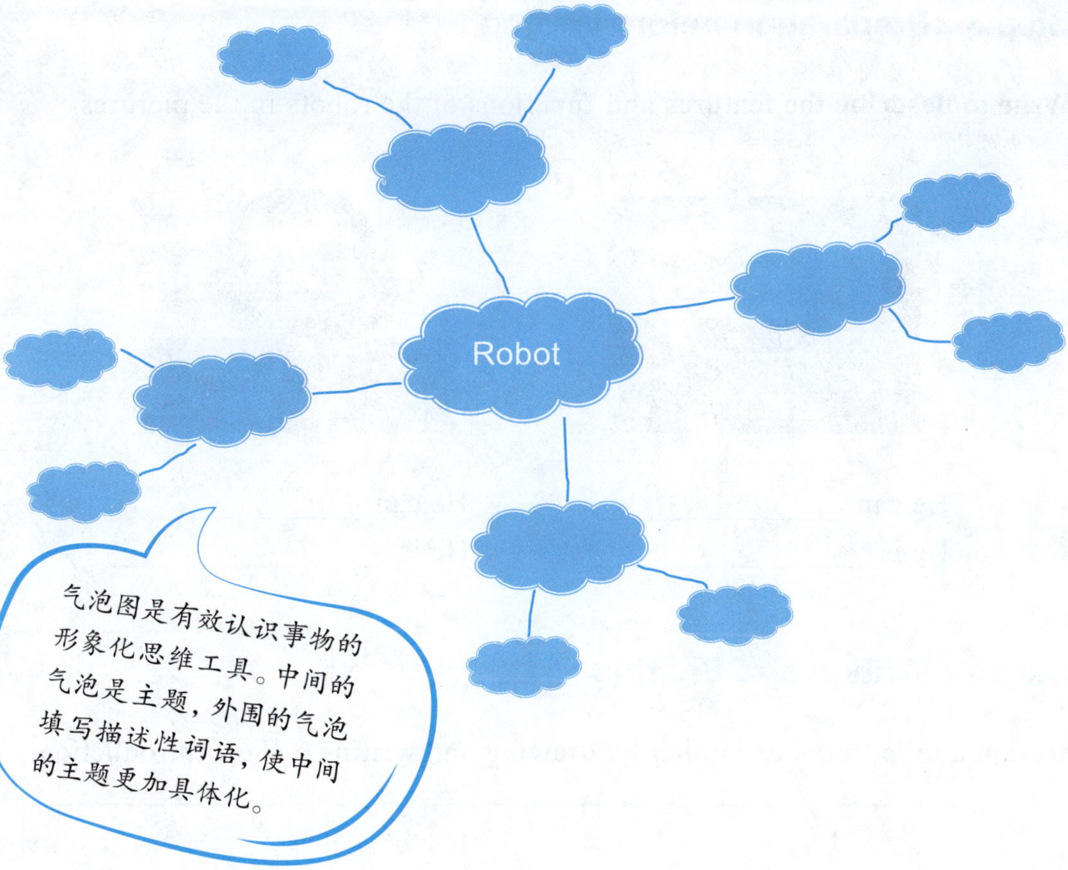

Step 2 Reading Comprehension

1. Read and **underline** the robot's name and his creator.
2. Read and **complete** the bubble map about Robin.

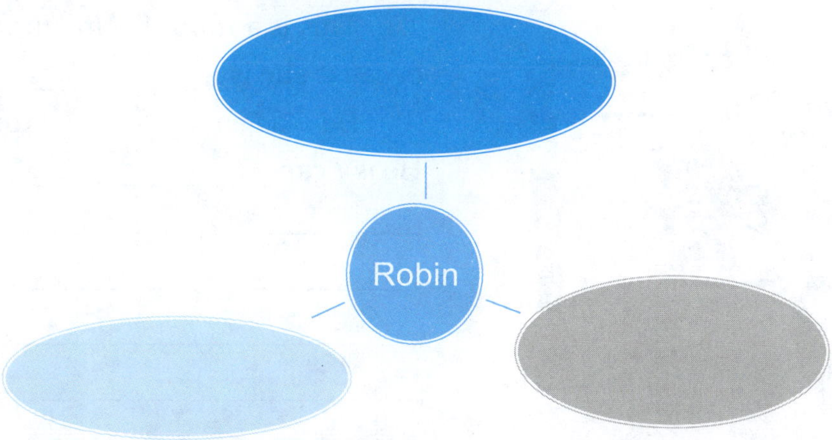

Step 3　Preparation before Writing

Write to **describe** the features and functions of the robots in the pictures.

He can ________________.
He is ________________.

He can ________________.
He is ________________.

Step 4　Writing and Sharing

Design a robot for your mother by drawing and writing a short introduction.

This is a robot for my mother because she is ____________.

He is a / an ____________ robot.

He is / can ____________________
____
____
____
____

教学时长: 1 hr

教学建议:

1. 读前准备环节。

教师引导学生回想描述外貌和性格特征的单词,鼓励学生运用相关词汇预测机器人(Robin)的特征和功能。

2. 阅读理解环节。

(1)教师引导学生运用跳读技巧快速找出机器人名字(Robin)和创造者(Grandpa)。

(2)教师引导学生阅读并提取关于机器人的特征和功能的信息,完成气泡图。

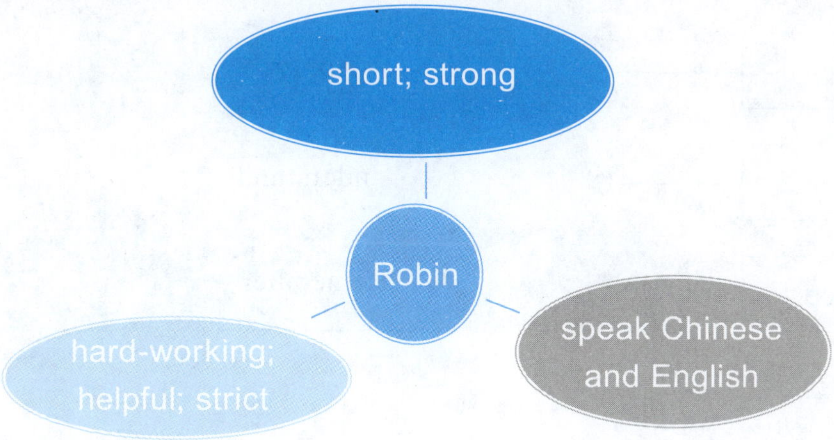

3. 写作准备环节。

教师引导学生观察机器人图片,学生用提供的句型描述机器人的外形和功能。

4. 写作与分享环节。

(1)教师将学生分为四人一组,组织学生讨论给妈妈设计的机器人应具备的特点和功能。

(2)教师引导学生观察图片,感受图片中妈妈的艰辛和忙碌。学生小组合作,以海报形式为妈妈设计机器人,用描写性格特征和功能的句型介绍所设计的机器人。

(3)教师可以采用"Gallery Walk"的形式让学生分享介绍设计出来的机器人。教师引导学生在分享过程中对比各自的机器人的功能,讨论为妈妈设计的机器人最重要的三个功能及理由,引导学生更好地理解母亲这一角色。

参考简介: This is a robot for my mother because she is very busy / tired / hard-working. He is a friendly robot. He can do the cleaning / washing / babysitting / cooking…

思维试纸:

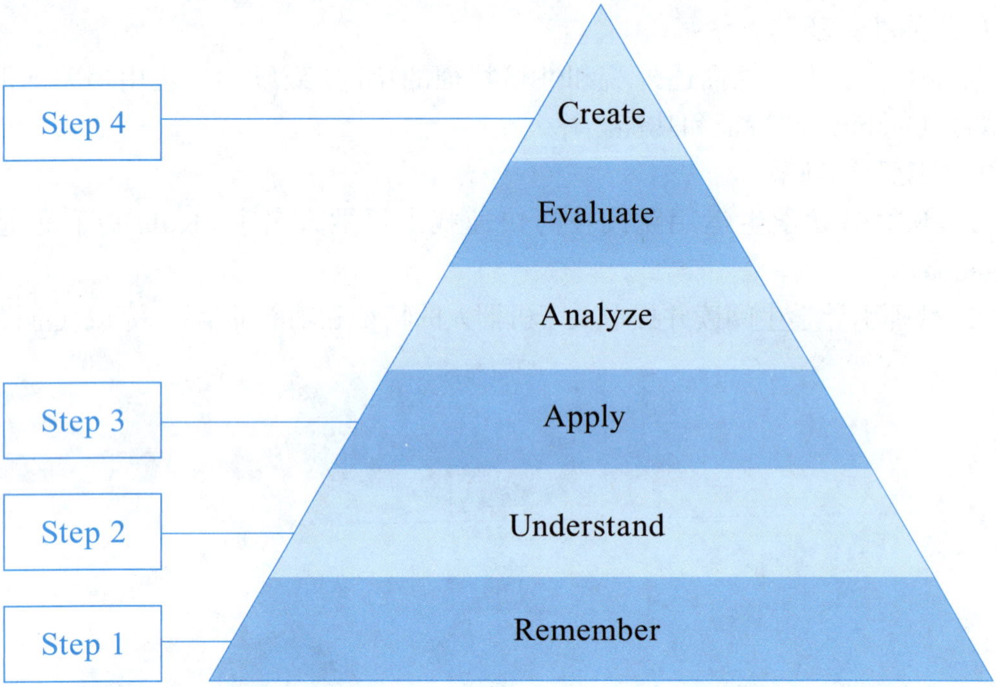

Part Three Vocabulary

教学素材: old, young, strict, funny, hard-working, helpful, clever, shy, polite, friendly, tall, short, strong, thin

教学步骤:

Step 1 Word Search

Circle the 5 words in this unit hidden in the word puzzle. The first one has been done for you.

b	a	u	m	i	n	t	o	n	d
w	h	e	l	p	f	u	l	z	i
c	h	y	e	t	a	h	a	l	f
s	e	o	s	y	f	u	n	n	y
t	z	u	e	a	t	r	a	k	e
r	n	n	l	d	i	n	g	o	r
i	c	g	t	i	v	e	h	u	e
c	j	w	o	k	e	p	t	l	n
t	r	a	s	h	y	a	r	d	t

Step 2 Word Pairs

Classify the words in the box into pairs.

Word Box

old	short	thin	clever	shy
lovely	tall	strong	young	out-going
smart	cute			

(1) ________ ________ (2) ________ ________ (3) ________ ________

(4) ________ ________ (5) ________ ________ (6) ________ ________

教学时长: 15 mins

教学建议:

词汇部分主要用于练习，旨在巩固词汇和语法知识。学生自行在课前或课后完成。课堂上，学生展示和分享作业，教师评价反馈，帮助学生正确理解并运用描述人物特征的形容词。

1. Step 1为圈词活动。教师引导学生从所给字母图表中圈出五个本单元所学的单词。

b	a	u	m	i	n	t	o	n	d
w	h	e	l	p	f	u	l	z	i
c	h	y	e	t	a	h	a	l	f
s	e	o	s	y	f	u	n	n	y
t	z	u	e	a	t	r	a	k	e
r	n	n	l	d	i	n	g	o	r
i	c	g	t	i	v	e	h	u	e
c	j	w	o	k	e	p	t	l	n
t	r	a	s	h	y	a	r	d	t

2. Step 2为单词配对活动。教师引导学生识别六组描述人物特征的反义词或近义词。

参考答案：(1) (反义词) old, young (2) (反义词) short, tall (3) (反义词) shy, out-going (4) (反义词) strong, thin (5) (近义词) lovely, cute (6) (近义词) smart, clever。

思维试纸：

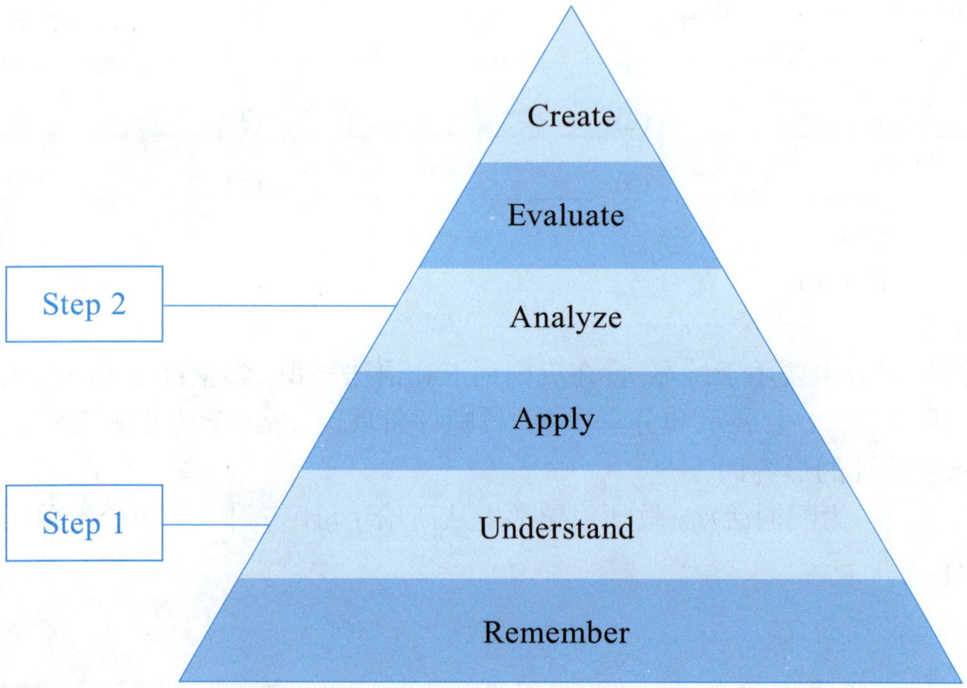

Part Four Grammar

教学素材: What's he / she like? He / She is…

教学步骤:

Step 1 Self-checking

Read the pictures (读图) below and **make** sentences (造句).

— What's ________ like?
— ________ is ________.

— What's ________ like?
— ________ is ________.

Step 2 Further Practicing

Select words or phrases to **match** the pictures.

— What's ________ like?
— ________ is ________.

— What's ________ like?
— ________ is ________.

— What's ________ like?
— ________ is ________.

a man	funny
30	shy
helpful	she
a woman	strong
hard-working	strict
he	

教学时长: 15 mins

教学建议:

语法部分主要用于练习，旨在巩固词汇和语法知识。学生自行在课前或课后完成，教师批改。课堂上，教师带领学生总结在使用目标句型时应注意人称代词“he / she”的区别，以及“is”后面应填写性格、外貌特征类形容词。教师可以引导学生仔细观察图片，运用尽可能多的形容词来描述图片中人物的特征。

1. 自我检测环节。

该部分要求学生根据图意完成句子，主要检测学生是否掌握重点句型：What's he / she like? He / She is…

参考答案：

What's she like? She is cute / lovely (short, friendly, shy).

What's he like? He is young (handsome, cool).

2. 巩固练习环节。

教师引导学生总结：本单元核心句型“What's he / she like? ”是对人物特征提问，回答该问题应使用形容词，而不使用名词。

参考答案：

(1) — What's he like?
— He is strong.

(2) — What's she like?
— She is strict and hard-working.

(3) — What's he like?
— He is funny.

思维试纸:

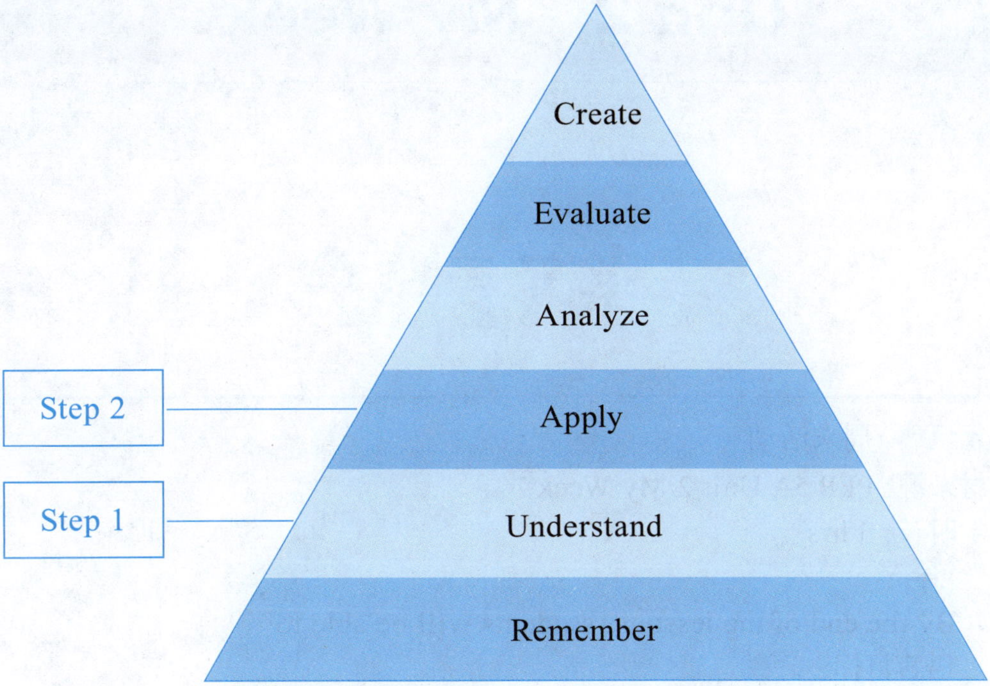
Create
Evaluate
Analyze
Apply
Understand
Remember
Step 2
Step 1

Unit 2 My Week

单元导览

单元话题: 周末活动
素材来源: PEP 5A Unit 2 My Week
教学时长: 3 hrs
教学目标:

By the end of the lessons, students will be able to

语言目标:

1. say and **recognize** the days of the week (Monday, Tuesday, Wednesday, Thursday, Friday, Saturday and Sunday) in English and talk about their subjects on weekdays;

2. **understand** and **use** the phrases (wash clothes, watch TV, do homework, read books and play football) to talk about their weekend activities;

3. **understand** the conversations in the textbook and discuss their weekend activities by **using** vocabulary about weekdays, subjects and activities in different situations;

4. **evaluate** their weekend activities and **design** a better weekend schedule for others.

非语言目标:

1. **optimize** their schedule, like how to arrange their free time properly;

2. work in groups to finish tasks related to their daily life about subjects and activities;

3. strengthen higher order thinking skills: **analyzing, evaluating** and **creating**;

4. **make** a proper weekend schedule with creative thinking and **judge** with critical thinking.

融思设计

Part One Listening and Speaking

教学素材: Part A Let's Talk
教学步骤:

Step 1 Listening Comprehension

1. **Predict** the lessons John has on Thursday and what Grandpa does on Thursday based on the picture in the textbook.

John has ____________ on Thursday.
Grandpa has ______________ on Thursday.

2. Listen and **fill in** the blanks.

John has ____________, ________ and ____________ on Thursday.

Grandpa has ________ on Thursday.

3. Listen again and **complete** the sentences.

____________ is John's ____________ teacher.
He is ____________.

Step 2 Preparing for Speaking

Read Wu Yifan's weekend schedule and **discuss** how he feels on the weekend and why.

Wu Yifan's Weekend Schedule

	Saturday	Sunday
9:00–11:00	Math	English
13:00–15:00	Handwriting	Art
18:00–20:00	Chinese Writing	Piano

— How does Wu Yifan feel on the weekend?
— I think he feels ________ on the weekend because...

Step 3 Speaking and Sharing

1. **Brainstorm** on the activities a good weekend schedule should have in groups.

A good weekend schedule should have ____________________.

2. Report your ideas to the whole class and **agree on** some key ideas.

A good weekend schedule should have ____________________.

3. **Identify** and circle what should be changed in the schedule.
4. **Change** the parts you identified with your group members and explain the reasons.

Language Kit

Wu Yifan has ______ on _______ before. Now we change it into ________________, because he likes _________.

He __________ on __________ before. Now we add _________, because ____________.

教学时长: 1.5 hrs

教学建议:

1. 听力理解环节。

(1) 教师引导学生通过仔细观察教材上图片中人物的穿着和周围环境，预测John周四上什么课，爷爷周四做什么，并完成句子填空。

(2) 教师播放录音，学生听录音并写出John周四上课科目和爷爷周四的活动安排。播放录音次数根据学生能力水平灵活处理。

(3) 教师再次播放录音，引导学生提取对话中其他重要信息：John的音乐老师姓名和性格特点。

Mr. Young is John's music teacher. He is funny.

2. 表达准备环节。

相关内容可安排学生在课前完成。

教师布置学生阅读吴一凡的周末安排，学生讨论这样的周末安排会让吴一凡做何感想。教师可以针对学生表达所需语言，提供相关词汇，比如tired, busy, interested, excited, angry, bored等。教师应对学生不熟悉的单词进行适当讲解。

3. 表达与分享环节。

(1) 学生分组开展头脑风暴，思考合理的周末安排应该包含的活动及理由。

（2）各小组向全班汇报对合理的周末安排的看法，教师引导学生正确认识如何合理安排周末时间，明确合理的周末安排要点，比如周末活动的类别、个人兴趣、劳逸结合、时间分配等。

（3）教师布置学生以小组为单位，根据第二步分享的内容，把自己认为吴一凡周末安排中不合理的地方圈起来，并思考如何改进。

（4）小组改进吴一凡的周末安排表，自愿向全班展示介绍新的周末安排表，并说明理由。

介绍示范：

Good morning, my dear classmates. It's our pleasure to introduce Wu Yifan's new weekend plan to you. Wu Yifan has handwriting on Saturday afternoon for 2 hours before. Now we change it into handwriting for 1 hour and playing basketball for 1 hour, because he likes sports.

思维试纸：

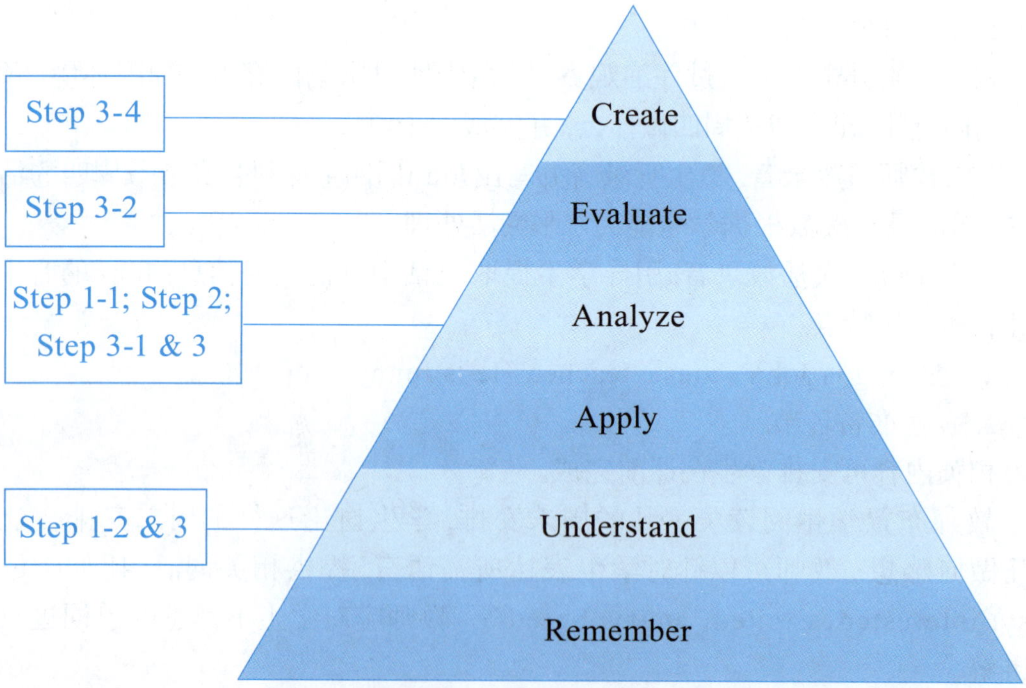

Part Two Reading and Writing

教学素材: Part B Read and Write
教学步骤:

Step 1 Learning before Reading

Read the pictures in the textbook and **tick** how Wu Yifan is feeling at the moment.

Wu Yifan is...

happy	☐	excited	☐	sad	☐	tired	☐
sleepy	☐	angry	☐	hungry	☐		

Step 2 Reading Comprehension

1. Read and **find out** what Wu Yifan is feeling at the moment and why.

Wu Yifan is ____________ because ____________.

2. Read and **tick** what he often or sometimes does on weekend and **cross** what he doesn't.

(1) do sports ☐ (2) watch TV ☐
(3) read books ☐ (4) play games ☐

3. **Evaluate** his schedule and decide what is good and what is not good.

It is good to have ____________ because ____________.

It is not good to have ____________ because ____________.

Step 3 Preparation before Writing

Compare the following schedule of an American primary school with yours, and put down the similarities and differences in the double bubble map.

Schedule					
	Monday	**Tuesday**	**Wednesday**	**Thursday**	**Friday**
8:50–9:00	Arrival	Arrival	Arrival	Arrival	Arrival
9:00–9:30	Morning Meeting	Morning Meeting	Morning Meeting	Morning Meeting	Morning Meeting
9:30–10:10	Math	Math	Math	Math	Spanish
10:10–10:55	Snack / Recess	Snack / Recess	Snack / Recess	Snack / Recess	Snack / Recess
10:55–11:25	Reading and Writing	Reading and Writing	Music	Reading and Writing	Reading and Writing
11:25–12:00	Reading and Writing	Reading and Writing	Spelling	Reading and Writing	Class Meeting
12:00–1:00	Lunch / Recess	Lunch / Recess	Lunch / Recess	Lunch / Recess	Lunch / Recess
1:00–1:30	Handwriting	Spelling	Handwriting	Spelling	Science
1:30–2:00	Class Meeting	Science	Science	Science	Science
2:00–2:45	Violin	Art	Dance	P.E.	Reading Partners
2:45–3:00	Pack up / Closing	Pack up / Closing	Pack up / Closing	Pack up / Closing	Pack up / Closing

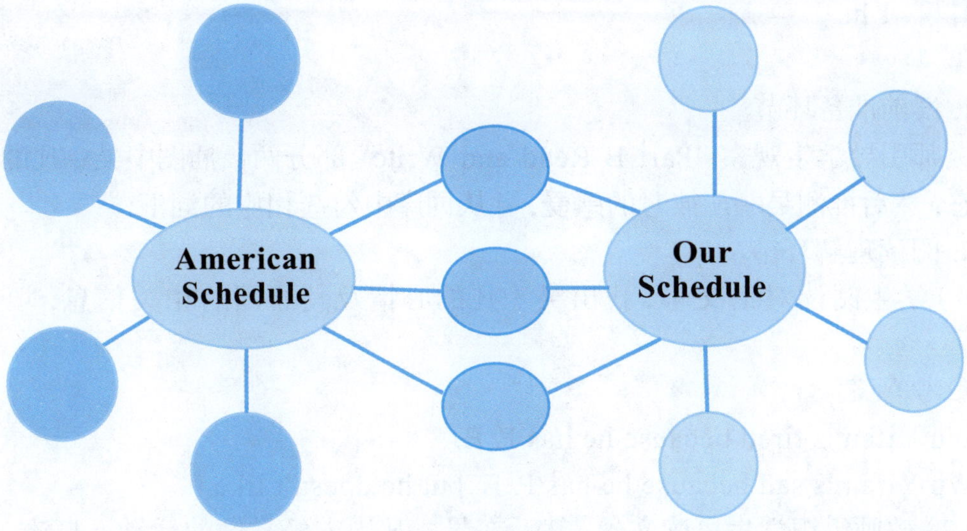

Step 4 Writing and Sharing

Write down at least 3 similarities and 3 differences between the two schedules.

Language Kit

We both have… (on…)

They have… on…, but we have…

They have… but we don't have…

教学时长: 1 hr

教学建议:

1. 读前准备环节。

教师引导学生观察"Part B Read and Write"部分两幅插图中吴一凡的表情和状态,然后推测吴一凡彼时的感受,并从词库中勾选相应的词汇。

2. 阅读理解环节。

(1)学生阅读对话文本,找出吴一凡的心情及其原因的相关信息,填入空白处。

参考答案:

Wu Yifan is tired because he has P. E.

Wu Yifan is sad because he has P. E. but he doesn't like it.

(2)教师组织学生再读文本,然后在吴一凡周末经常做的活动下打钩,周末不会做的活动下打叉。

(3)教师引导学生根据听说活动中制定的合理安排周末活动的标准对吴一凡的周末活动安排进行评价,并说明理由,比如周末应该加强运动锻炼,保持身体健康。教师可以进一步鼓励学生就周末适合做什么运动提出建议。

3. 写作准备环节。

教师首先向学生介绍美国小学课表,适当讲解拓展课表安排的相关知识,比如"Snack / Recess"是点心/休息时间,"Reading and Writing"类似于我们的语文课,"Spanish"是外语课,"Reading Partners"是阅读分享活动。然后,教师引导学生将美国小学课表与自己的课表进行对比,找出两者之间的异同,并填入双气泡图。教师可以引导学生从课程类型、课程安排等方面思考。

4. 写作与分享环节。

教师引导学生选择双气泡图中呈现的3点相似之处和3点不同之处进行写作。教师可以引导学生运用所给句型,并适当举例。

写作示例:

We both have math on Monday, Tuesday and Friday.

We both have a foreign language subject.

We both have class meeting.

They have dance but we don't.

They have five science lessons but we just have one.

They have morning meeting every day but we just have it on Monday.

教师还可以根据学生水平进一步引导学生关注中美小学课表的差异,比如他们上学时间更晚,放学时间更早,两节课之间没有课间休息等。

思维试纸:

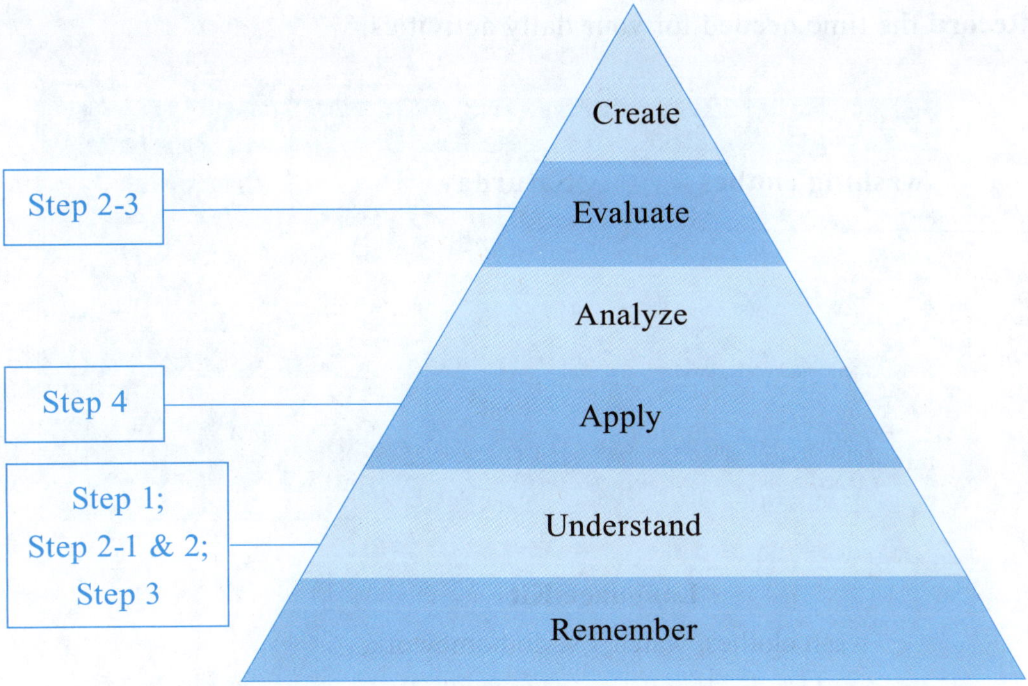

Part Three Vocabulary

教学素材: wash clothes, watch TV, do homework, read books and play football

教学步骤:

Step 1 Self-checking

Choose the correct words in brackets to complete the following sentences.

(1) The two kids are (washing / watching) TV.

(2) Anna is (looking / washing) clothes.

(3) I often (read / look) books on the weekend.

(4) Do you like (playing / reading) football?

(5) My classmates sometimes (do / make) homework in the classroom.

Step 2 My Daily Activities

1. **Record** the time needed for your daily activities.

Activity	Day	Time Needed
washing clothes	Saturday	20 minutes

Language Kit

wash clothes, watch TV, do homework,
read books, have class, play football

2. **Arrange** the activities from the most time needed to the least and decide whether it is good or not.

1. ______ 2. ______ 3. ______ 4. ______ 5. ______ 6. ______

I spend... (花费的时间) on... I think it is (not) good.

教学时长: 15 mins

教学建议:

词汇部分主要用于练习，旨在巩固词汇和语法知识。学生自行在课前或课后完成，教师课堂上评价反馈，并引导学生总结存在的问题和解决办法，注重巩固学生对本单元重点单词词性、词义的理解。

The two kids are **watching** TV.

Anna is **washing** clothes.

I often **read** books on the weekend.

Do you like **playing** football?

My classmates sometimes **do** homework in the classroom.

1. Step 1 是短语匹配活动，主要检测学生对本单元核心短语的理解。教师可以根据学生水平适当复习，然后引导学生根据句意，选择正确的词汇完成句子。

2. Step 2: 教师需引导学生根据自己的实际情况填写日常活动，包括上课、洗衣服、吃饭、睡觉、运动、娱乐、做作业、阅读等，并大致记录每项活动花费的时间。学生根据所花费时间长短将活动进行排序，并反思时间安排是否合理，从而对自己日常活动的时间安排有进一步认识，提升合理安排日常生活的意识。

思维试纸:

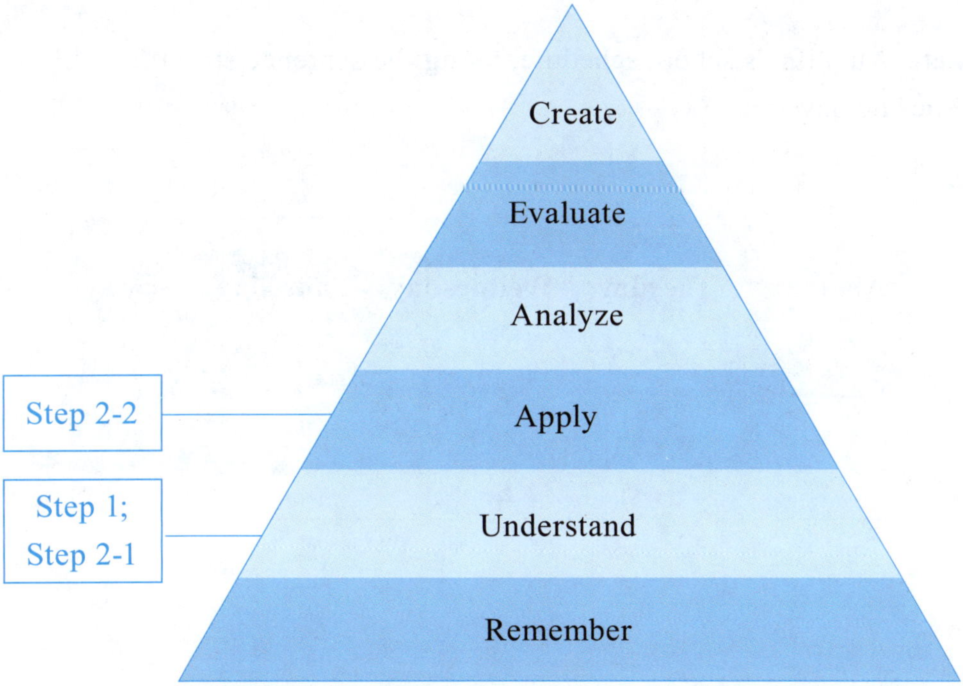

Part Four Grammar

教学素材: What do you have on…? / I have… / What does he / she have on…? / He / She has…

教学步骤:

Step 1 Self-checking

Complete the sentences based on your school schedule.

What do you have in a week?

I have ________, _________, and ________ on Wednesday.

I have English on _________, __________, and ______________.

I have ______________ every day.

What do you do in a week?

I _____________________ on _____________________.

I _____________________ every day.

Step 2 Information Gap Activity

Complete Wu Yifan's school schedule, **using** the sentence structures:

What does he have on…?

He has…

Monday	Tuesday	Wednesday	Thursday	Friday

A版

Monday	Tuesday	Wednesday	Thursday	Friday
Science	Chinese	Math	Art	English

B版

Monday	Tuesday	Wednesday	Thursday	Friday
Math	English	Chinese	P.E.	Computer

教学时长: 15 mins

教学建议:

1. 语法部分主要用于对话练习中，旨在帮助学生正确运用本单元重点句型“What do you have on…? / I have…/ What does he / she have on…? / He / She has…”。教师需要注意学生是否能完成人称和助动词的变化。

2. 信息沟交际活动：学生两人一组，教师在课堂上将A、B版课表分别发给两个同学，并要求其通过运用重点句型问答，获取课表中空缺的课程信息，完成吴一凡的课表。

Monday	Tuesday	Wednesday	Thursday	Friday
Math	English	Chinese	P.E.	Computer
Science	Chinese	Math	Art	English

思维试纸:

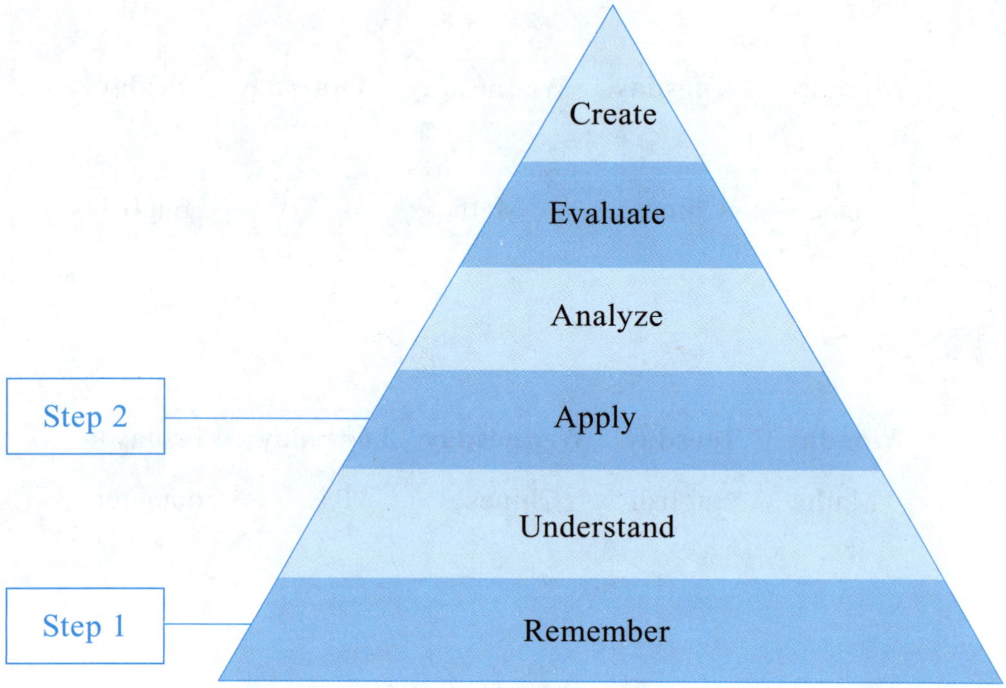
Create
Evaluate
Analyze
Step 2
Apply
Understand
Step 1
Remember

Unit 3 What Would You Like?

单元导览

单元话题: 食物
素材来源: PEP 5A Unit 3 What Would You Like?
教学时长: 3 hrs
教学目标:

By the end of the lessons, students will be able to

语言目标:

1. **name** the five foods (sandwich, salad, hamburger, ice cream, and tea) in English and **describe** their features by associating words, such as fresh, health, delicious, hot and sweet;

2. **understand** conversations in the textbook and discuss what they would like in the restaurant by **using** vocabulary about food;

3. order food by **using** sentence patterns: What would you like? / I'd like...

4. **comprehend** the meaning of the note, **analyze** the main content and structure, and **apply** the knowledge and language to **writing** a note to Robin about the food they would like.

非语言目标:

1. **associate** health knowledge with food ordering;

2. work in groups to **finish** tasks related to the food they would like;

3. **understand** the importance of a healthy diet;

4. strengthen higher order thinking skills: **analyzing**, **evaluating** and **creating**;

5. **design** menus with creative thinking and **judge** with critical thinking.

融思设计

Part One Listening and Speaking

教学素材: Part A Let's Talk
教学步骤:

Step 1 Listening Comprehension

Listen and **complete** the form.

Who	What would he / she like to eat? Why?	What would he / she like to drink? Why?

Step 2 Preparation before Speaking

Read the menu and **make** an order for the 2 children.

Food	Drink
sandwich	tea
hamburger	water
salad	Cola
ice cream	milk
noodles	juice
beef	coffee
fruits	
vegetables	
chicken	

My Order

Food:

Drink:

Step 3 Speaking and Sharing

1. Discuss and **evaluate** the food in your order with group members and **decide** the final order in your group.

Language Kit

What would you like?

I'd like some… for…

It is good for you because it is delicious / healthy / children's favorite.

2. **Share** the final order of your group to the class.

This is our order for the 2 children. We'd like some… for… because she / he is… and it is…

教学时长: 1.5 hrs

教学建议:

1. 听力理解环节。

教师播放录音，要求学生听对话并找出关键信息填入表格：人物、想吃的食物、想喝的饮料以及原因。

Who	What would he / she like to eat? Why?	What would he / she like to drink? Why?
Father	A sandwich. Because he is hungry.	He'd like some water because he is thirsty.

2. 表达准备环节。

教师引导学生观察两张图片，了解图片中的人物和情境。学生阅读菜单并为两位小朋友点餐，然后将所点的食物和饮品单词写入“My Order”活动单中。

3. 表达与分享环节。

（1）教师将学生分为3~4人一组，讨论询问彼此的点餐情况，并评价所点的食物和饮品是否恰当。

（2）教师可以先做口语表达示范，询问一位同学的点餐情况，并引导其他同学从味道、健康以及个人喜好等方面评价点餐是否恰当。

（3）小组讨论并就点餐达成一致意见，完成小组的点餐并分享给全班同学。分享时建议教师或全班同学提问，小组回答。

This is our order for the 2 children. We'd like some juice for the boy because he is thirsty and it is healthy with Vitamin C. And we'd like some beef for him because he likes meat. Then, we'd like some hamburger and ice cream for the girl because she likes fast food and desserts.

思维试纸:

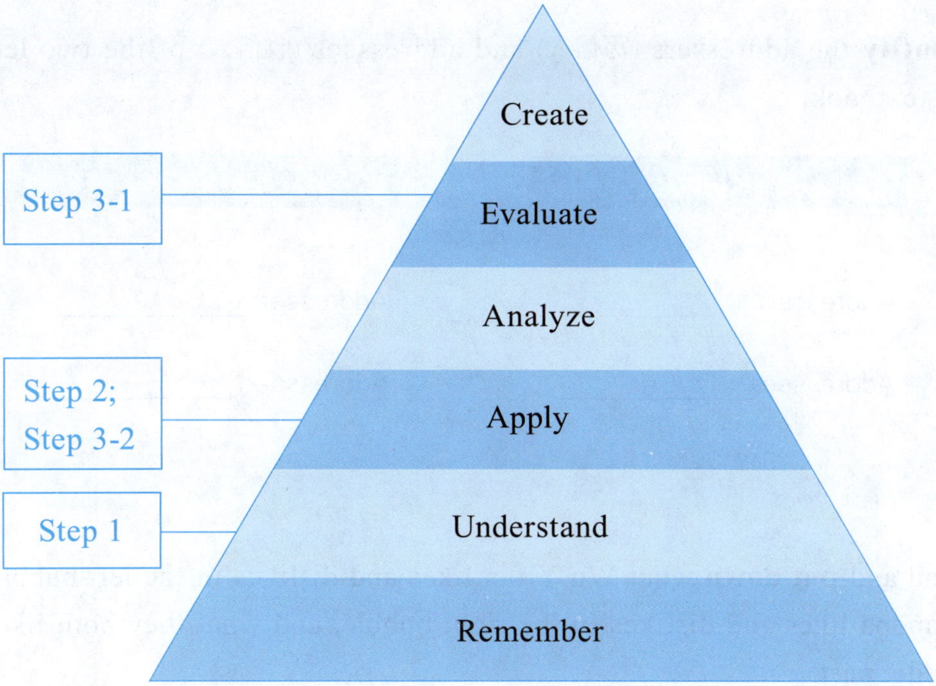

Part Two Reading and Writing

教学素材: Part B Read and Write
教学步骤:

Step 1 Preparation before Reading

Rank the following food from what you like least to most.

chicken	beef	fish	salad
hamburger	sandwich	juice	tea

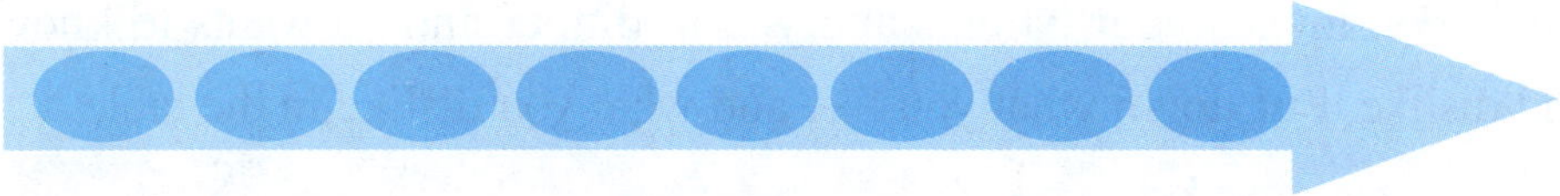

Step 2 Reading Comprehension

1. **Identify** the addressers (写信人) and addressees (收信人) of the two letters in the textbook.

Letter 1

Addresser: ____________

Addressee: ____________

Letter 2

Addresser: ____________

Addressee: ____________

2. Read and **put down** what Wu Yifan likes and dislikes in the left bubble, what Grandpa likes and dislikes in the right bubble, and what they both like in the middle part.

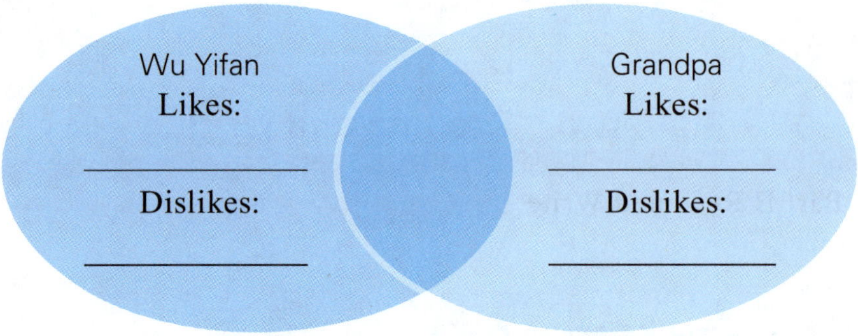

3. **Think about** why they say no to Robin's dish.

   They say no because ______________________________.

Step 3 Preparation before Writing

Your friend Simon invites your parents and you to dinner and he wants to know what you like and dislike. **Put down** what you like and what you dislike in the table.

Who	Likes	Dislikes

Step 4 Writing and Sharing

Write a letter to Simon and tell him what your family would like to eat and drink and what you would not like and give reasons.

Language Kit

I don't like to eat / drink... but... is OK.

I like to eat / drink... but not...

Dear __________,

____

____

____

Thank you!

____

____

教学时长: 1 hr

教学建议:

1. 读前准备环节。

教师引导学生根据自己的饮食喜好将列举出的食物、饮品按照从最不喜欢到最喜欢的顺序排序，并将相应的单词填入图表圈内。

2. 阅读理解环节。

（1）教师引导学生关注阅读文本的文体特点，运用跳读和寻读技巧找出两封信的写信人和收信人。

Letter 1

Addresser: Wu Yifan　　　　Addressee: Robin

Letter 2

Addresser: Grandpa　　　　Addressee: Robin

（2）学生阅读信件文本，勾画吴一凡和爷爷喜欢和不喜欢吃的食物，并将信息填入圆圈图，分别呈现吴一凡和爷爷喜欢和不喜欢吃的食物，以及他们俩都喜欢吃的食物。

Wu Yifan likes ice cream, onion and salad. Wu Yifan doesn't like beef.

Grandpa likes chicken and vegetables. Grandpa doesn't like carrots.

They both like onions.

（3）教师引导学生思考为什么吴亦凡和爷爷不喜欢Robin做的食物，并把答案填写在横线上。

3. 写作准备环节。

教师创设情境：你的朋友Simon邀请你及家人吃饭，想提前了解你们喜欢和不喜欢吃的食物。教师引导学生将相关信息填入表格。

4. 写作与分享环节。

教师引导学生熟悉如何表达喜欢或不喜欢的某种食物。学生根据写作准备环节中填写的食物的喜好信息写信给Simon，告知他自己喜欢和不喜欢的食物。教师可以关注学生是否能正确填写收信人和写信人信息。

信件示例：

Dear Simon,

My favorite food is beef. It is delicious and nutritious. Vegetables are OK, but I don't like onions. I also like juice but not cider.

Thank you!

思维试纸:

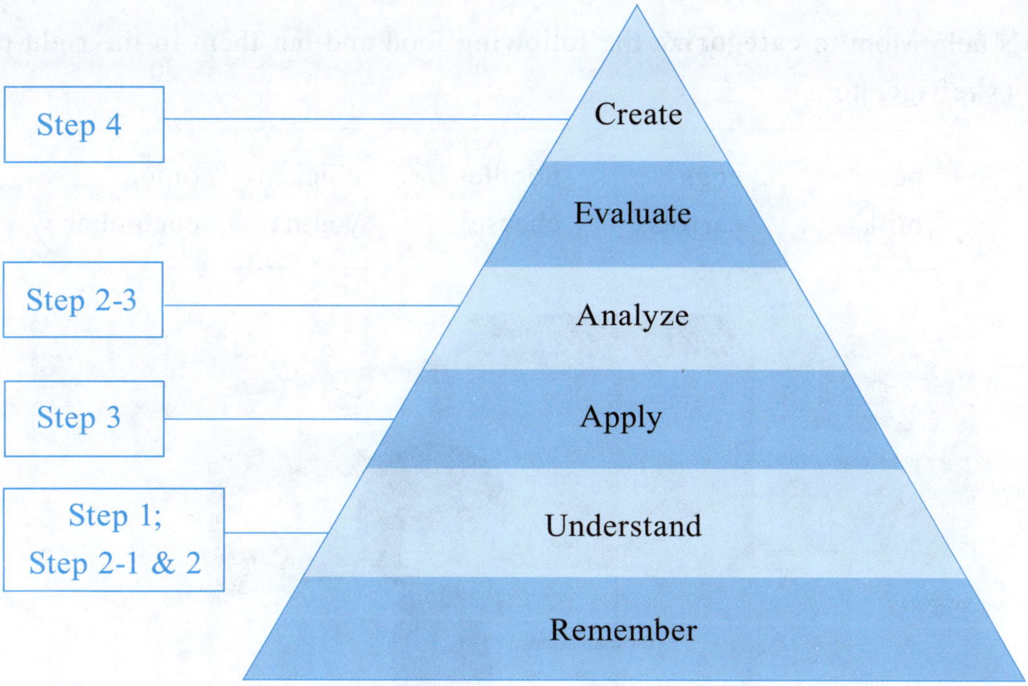

Part Three Vocabulary

教学素材: ice cream, tea, hamburger, sandwich, salad, fresh, healthy, delicious, hot and sweet

教学步骤:

Step 1 Self-checking

Fill in the blanks with appropriate letters to complete the words.

(1) Hamb__ __ ger is d__l__cious.

(2) S__l__d is fre__ __ and h__ __lthy.

(3) Sandwi__ __ is deli__ __ous.

(4) __ __ __ cream is sw__ __t.

(5) T__a is h__t.

Step 2 My Refrigerator

Let's help Mom to **categorize** the following food and put them in the right part of her refrigerator.

beef	eggs	noodles	chicken	onion
milk	carrots	cheese	yogurt	cucumber

Step 3 My Cooking

Decide what ingredients (配料) are needed for the dishes and put down appropriate words in the blanks.

chicken hamburger ______________

beef noodles ______________

vegetable salad ______________

egg sandwich ______________

教学时长：15 mins

教学建议：

词汇部分主要用于练习，旨在巩固本单元所学词汇和语法知识。学生可自行在课前或课后完成，教师评价反馈。课堂上，教师带领学生总结存在的问题和解决办法，注重巩固学生对本单元重点单词词性、词义的理解。

1. Step 1：学生复习单词的书写，将单词缺少的部分填写在横线上。

参考答案：

(1) Hamburger is delicious.

(2) Salad is fresh and healthy.

(3) Sandwich is delicious.

(4) Ice cream is sweet.

(5) Tea is hot.

2. Step 2 考查学生对食物的分类能力和生活常识。教师可以联系生活设置情境，比如帮助妈妈将购买的食物分门别类放入冰箱并说明理由。教师可以根据活动需要和学生水平补充冰箱主要储物空间的英文单词，比如蛋架（egg rack / tray）、层架（shelf）、冷冻室（freezer compartment）、冷藏室（fridge compartment）。

参考答案：

冷藏室第一层：noodles, milk, cheese, yogurt

冷藏室第二层：onion, carrots, cucumber

冷冻室：beef, chicken

蛋架：eggs

3. Step 3 考查学生对菜式原料的认识。教师可以引导学生根据自己的口味和喜好选择能做出不同菜式的原料，充分发挥学生的创造力和想象力。

参考答案：

chicken hamburger: chicken, bread, lettuce, salad sauce, etc.

beef noodles: beef, noodles, soybean sauce, pepper, salt, etc.

vegetable salad: onion, lettuce, tomato, red pepper, salad sauce, cucumber, etc.

egg sandwich: egg, toast, cheese, salad sauce, cucumber, etc.

思维试纸：

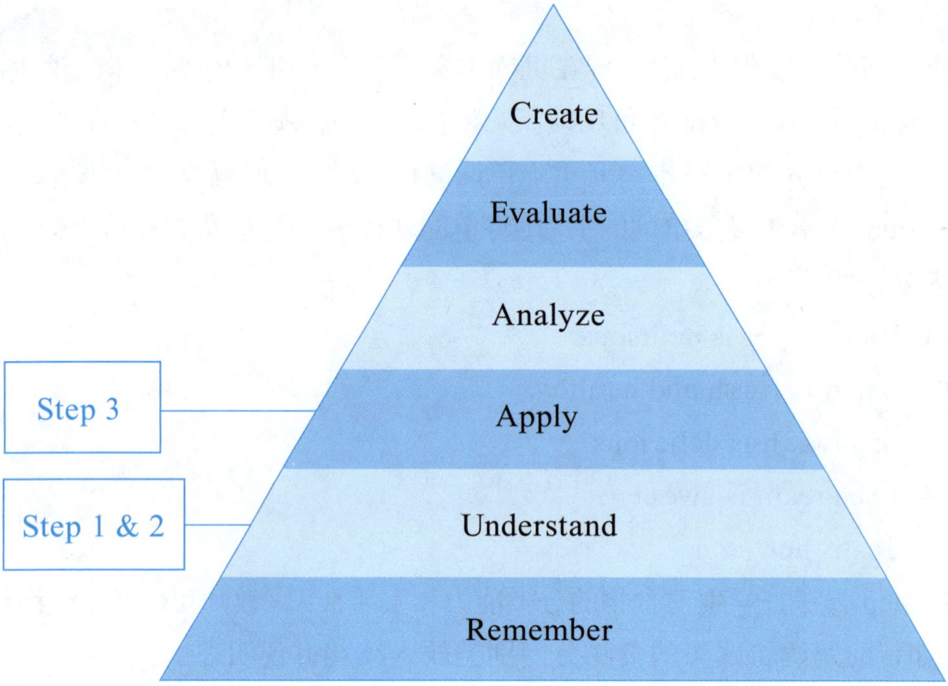

Part Four Grammar

教学素材：What would you / he / she like? / I / He / She would like to eat / drink…

What do you like? / I like… / I don't like…, because it's…

教学步骤：

Step 1 Self-checking

Complete the sentences with appropriate words.

(1) — What ________ you like ________?
— I'd like some noodles.

(2) — What ______ you like ________?
— I'd like some water.

(3) — What ________ you like?
— I like vegetables but not carrots.

Step 2 Rule-finding

Summarize the sentence patterns for the functions.

Ordering food and drink: ________________

Expressing likes or dislikes: ________________

Step 3 Further Practicing

Find out what the people in the pictures would like to eat / drink according to the given information.

She'd like __________.　She'd like __________.　He'd like __________.

教学时长：15 mins

教学建议：

1. 语法部分旨在巩固学生对重点句型的使用，本单元重点句型为 "What would you like to eat / drink? / I'd like..."。教师引导学生注意区别 "What do you like?" 和 "What would you like to eat / drink?"。前者主要用于询问喜欢什么，后者用于询问想吃（喝）什么。

参考答案：

(1) What would you like to eat?

(2) What would you like to drink?

(3) What do you like?

2. 学生可自行在课前或课后完成，也可在课堂上进行练习，教师可引导学生归纳询问想吃（喝）什么以及喜欢什么两种功能的句型，总结存在的问题和解决办法。

Ordering food and drink:

What would you like to eat / drink?

I'd like...

Expressing likes:

What do you like? / What's your favorite...?

I like...

I don't like...

I like... but not...

3. 教师引导学生根据人物介绍为他们提供恰当的食品和饮品，注意帮助学生区分“I'd like...”和“I like...”两个句型。

思维试纸：

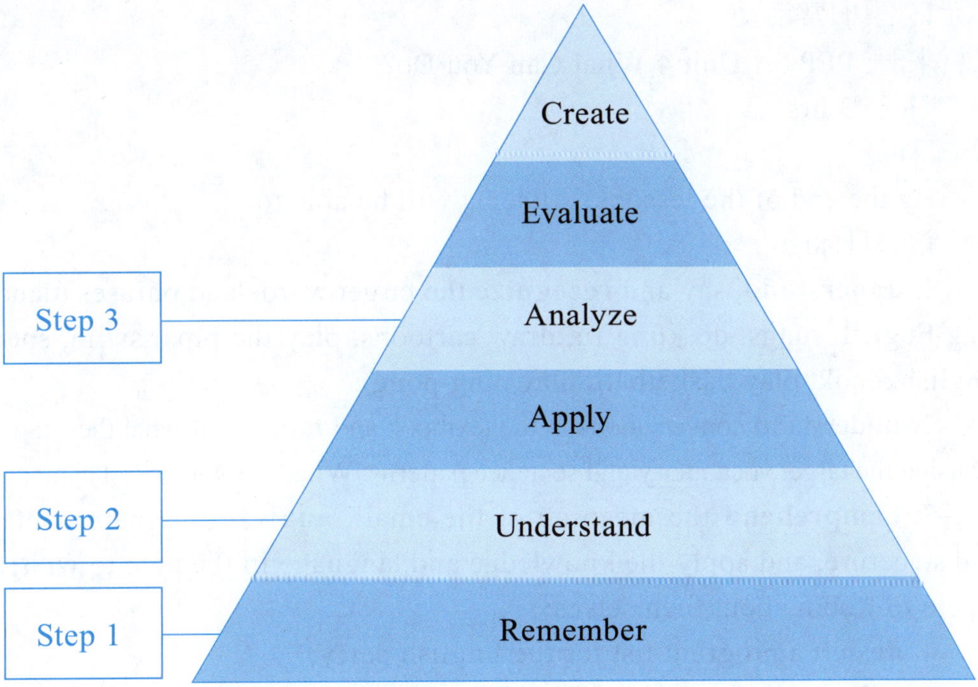

Unit 4 What Can You Do?

单元导览

单元话题: 日常活动
素材来源: PEP 5A Unit 4 What Can You Do?
教学时长: 3 hrs
教学目标:

By the end of the lessons, students will be able to

语言目标:

1. **understand**, say and **recognize** the target words and phrases (dance, sing English songs, do kung fu, draw cartoons, play the pipa, swim, speak English, cook, play basketball, play ping-pong);

2. **understand** conversations in the textbook and **talk about** what they can do by using the target vocabulary and sentence patterns: What can you do? / I can…

3. **comprehend** the meaning of the email, **analyze** the main content and structure, and apply the knowledge and language in the note to **writing** a note to Robin about themselves;

4. **design** a program list for the English party;

5. **write** an email to Robin to introduce themselves and tell what they can do;

6. share emails in groups to **decide on** who is the best one to be Robin's friend.

非语言目标:

1. work in groups to finish tasks related to what people can or can't do;

2. **know** more about their own and their classmates' talents;

3. strengthen their higher order thinking skills: **analyzing**, **evaluating** and **creating**;

4. **design** a program list for the English party with creative thinking and **judge** with critical thinking.

融思设计

Part One Listening and Speaking

教学素材: Part A Let's Talk
教学步骤:

Step 1 Listening Comprehension

Listen and **fill in** the blanks.

(1) Zhang Peng can ______________. (2) John can ______________.

Step 2 Preparation before Speaking

1. **Find out** what your group members can do for the English party.

Name	Can

2. **Design** a program list for a one-hour English party for the National Day celebration based on the table you just filled.

English Party

Grade: ________ Class: ________ Date: ________ Time: ________

Program	Performer(s)	Time

By Group ________

Step 3 Speaking and Sharing

1. **Share** your English party program list to the class.
2. **Evaluate** and vote for your favorite one and explain the reasons.

Language Kit

I think my favorite one is ___________ because __________.

教学时长: 1.5 hrs

教学建议:

1. 听力理解环节。

教师播放录音, 学生听录音找出张鹏和 John 能在班级英语晚会上表演的节目并填空。教师根据学生完成情况可再播放一遍录音, 并进行校对。

Zhang Peng can sing English songs.

John can do some kung fu.

2. 表达准备环节。

(1) 教师将学生分为4~5人一组, 小组成员相互询问能在英语晚会上表演的节目, 并填入表格。

(2) 小组根据各自才艺讨论制定时长为1个小时的国庆英语晚会节目单, 包括节目名称、表演者以及节目时长。

3. 表达与分享环节。

教师邀请各小组展示自己的英语晚会节目单, 并制定评价标准, 投票推选最佳节目单。评价标准可以考虑节目的多样性、节目名称等。教师可以根据活动需要和学生水平补充相关形容词, 比如exciting, interesting, special, awesome, great等。

参考示例:

I think my favorite program is the English song *Yesterday Once More* because it is a classic English song and I like it.

思维试纸:

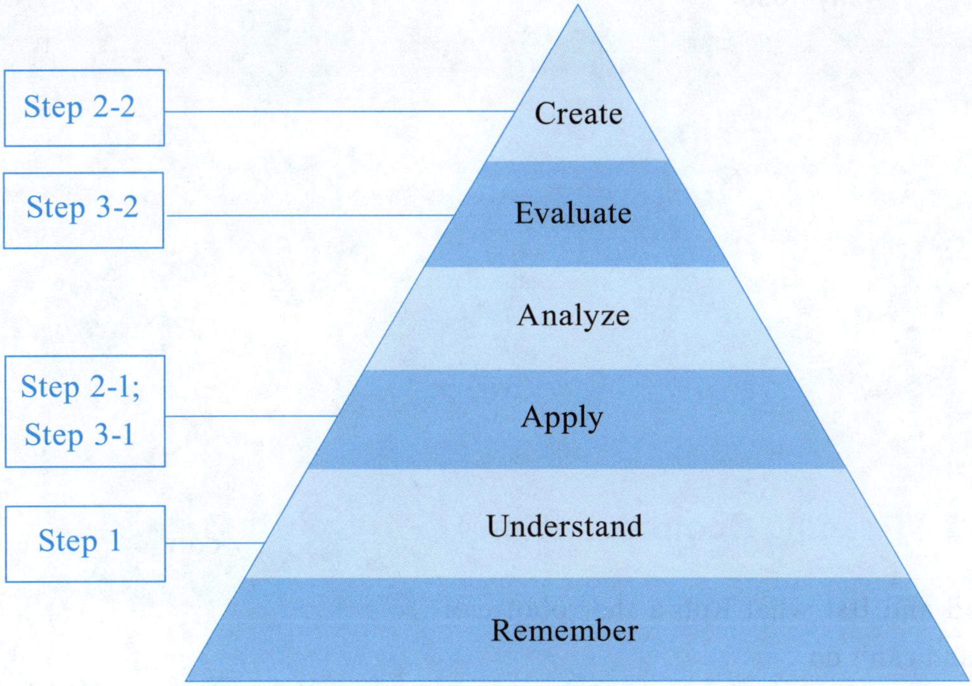

Part Two Reading and Writing

教学素材: Part B Read and Write

教学步骤:

Step 1 Preparation before Reading

1. Chain Game: I can do it!

Students work in groups to **act out** what different animals can do with body language and ask if the one sitting next can do it.

— I am a penguin and I can turn my head. Can you do it?

— Yes, I can.

2. Supposing you have a robot, draw what it is like and **fill in** the bubble map with what it can do.

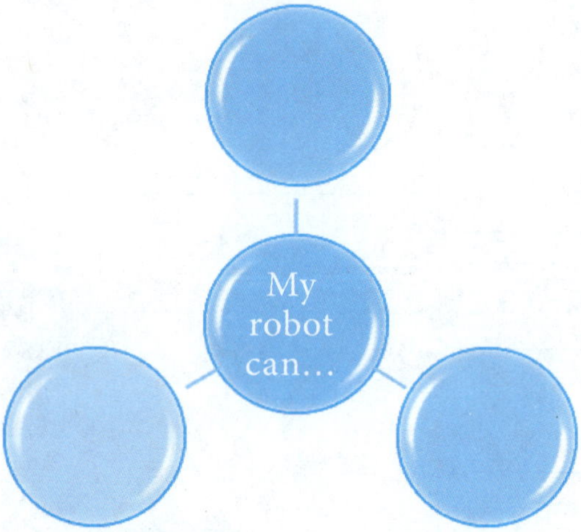

Step 2　Reading Comprehension

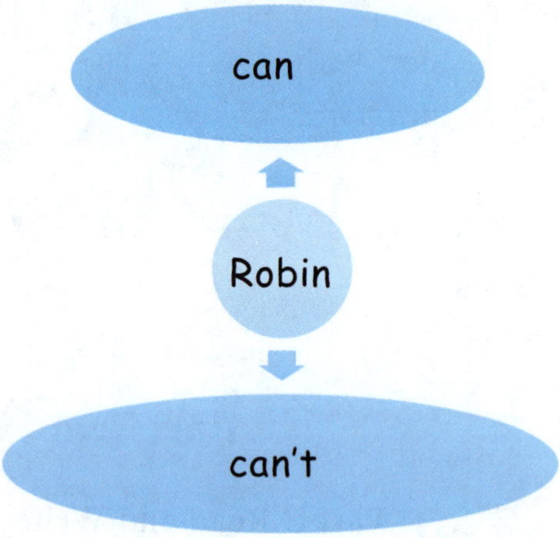

1. Read and **list** what Robin the robot can do and can't do.

2. **Compare** Robin with your robot, and complete the double bubble map to present the similarities and differences.

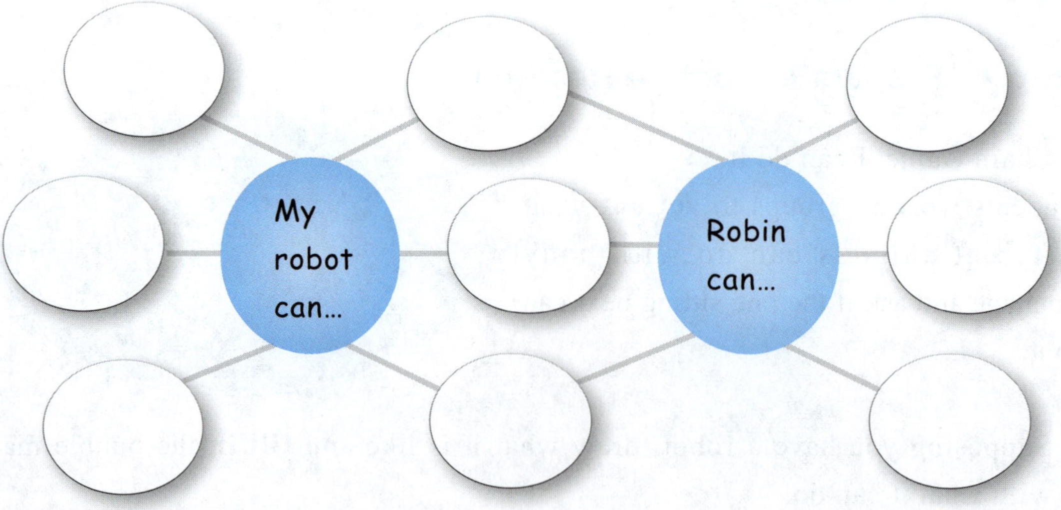

Step 3 Preparation before Writing

Good friends should have something in common. Talk to your deskmate and see if you can **find** 3 things that you and your deskmate both can do and neither can do in the chart. If you can, you can be good friends.

We both can

______

______

______

Neither of us can

______

______

______

Step 4 Writing and Sharing

1. **Write down** the things both your deskmate and you can do.

2. **Write** an email to one of your classmates to tell him / her 3 things that you can't do and ask him / her for help.

______ and I can be good friends because both of us can ______.

Dear ______,

______

______

______

______

______

Yours,

______

教学时长: 1 hr

教学建议:

1. 读前准备环节。

(1) 教师通过 "Chain Game" 帮助学生复习本单元目标词汇以及学过的动词或动词短语。教师引导学生思考不同的动物擅长做什么不同的动作, 具体内容可以参考绘本 *From Head to Toe*。

I'm a giraffe and I can bend my neck.

I'm a gorilla and I can thump my chest.

I'm an elephant and I can stomp my foot.

I'm a donkey and I can kick my legs.

(2) 学生想象自己有一个机器人, 在左边方框里画出它的样子, 在右边气泡图里列举它的特殊功能。

2. 阅读理解环节。

(1) 学生阅读Robin的邮件, 找出它能做和不能做的事情。

参考答案:

Robin can speak English and Chinese, do some kung fu and play ping-pong.

Robin can't swim.

(2) 学生对比Robin和自己的机器人, 运用双气泡图呈现两者之间的相似和不同之处。

3. 写作准备环节。

教师向学生介绍好朋友应该有共同点, 引导学生两人一组进行交流, 询问彼此擅长做的事, 如果能找到三件及以上两人都能做或都不能做的事, 他们就可能成为好朋友。根据学生情况, 教师可以补充相关词汇。

4. 写作与分享环节。

(1) 教师引导学生将两人都能做的三件事填入心形文本框, 祝贺他们可能成为好朋友。

(2) 教师引导学生仿写教材中的邮件, 给同学发一封邮件, 介绍自己不擅长做的事, 寻求帮助。

思维试纸:

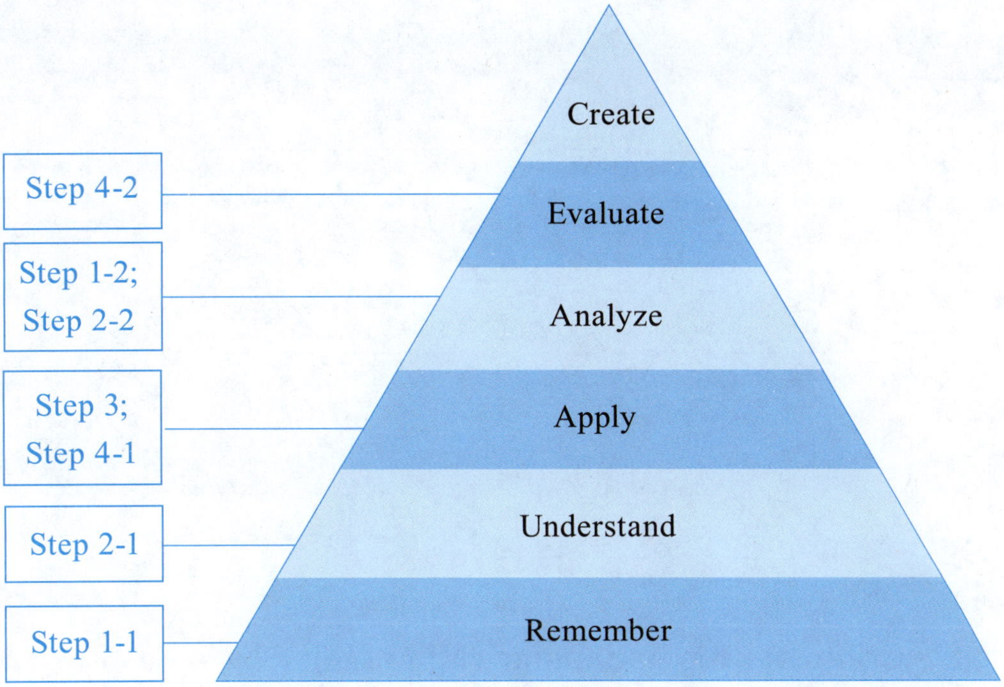

Part Three Vocabulary

教学素材: dance, sing English songs, do kung fu, draw cartoons, play the pipa, swim, speak English, cook, play basketball, play ping-pong, play football, play the piano

教学步骤:

Step 1 Let's Bingo!

dance	sing English songs	do kung fu
draw cartoons	play the pipa	swim
speak English	play basketball	cook
play ping-pong	play football	play the piano

Step 2 Complete the Vocabulary Mind Map

教学时长: 15 mins

教学建议:

词汇部分主要用于练习，旨在巩固词汇和语法知识。Step 1在课堂上完成，Step 2可以安排学生自行在课前或课后完成，教师批改或在课堂上分享展示，并针对存在的问题进行补充讲解。

1. Step 1为“Bingo”词汇游戏。教师引导学生从词汇列表中任意选择九个单词或短语填入九宫格的任意位置内，然后教师任意念出列表中的单词或短语，如果学生九宫格内有这个单词，就用“×”划去，没有就等下一个。第一个将横、竖、斜任意一个方向的格子连成一条线的学生大声说出“Bingo”，赢得比赛。教师可以适当给予一定的奖励。教师也可以进行两到三轮，让更多的学生能赢得比赛，巩固学生对所学单词或短语音和形的理解。

2. Step 2 主要是巩固拓展学生对短语中动词搭配的掌握。教师引导学生完成两个词汇思维图，一个是以“play”为动词的短语，另一个是以“do”为动词的短语。教师可以举例，帮助学生理解如何完成该活动。该活动答案不唯一，教师可以鼓励学生自主学习，提供更多相关搭配的短语。

参考答案：

play basketball, play football, play ping-pong, play badminton, play tennis, play the piano, play the pipa, play the violin, etc.

do kung fu, do homework, do a good job, do cooking, do cleaning, do washing, etc.

思维试纸：

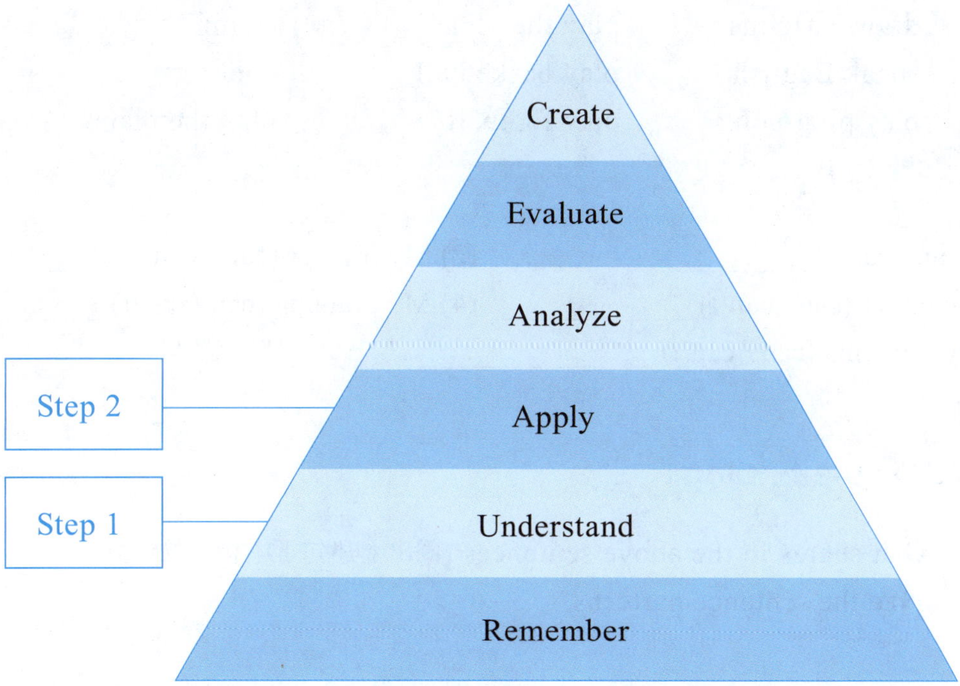

Part Four　Grammar

教学素材: What can you do? / I can / can't…
教学步骤:

Step 1　Self-checking

Make sentences to share if you and your family members can do the things listed in the box.

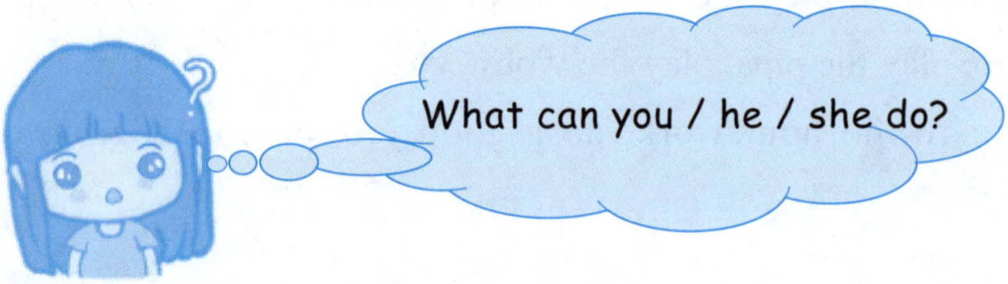

dance	sing English songs	do kung fu
draw cartoons	play the pipa	swim
speak English	play basketball	cook
play ping-pong	play football	play the piano

(1) I (can / can't) __________.　(2) My mother (can / can't) ___________.
(3) My father (can / can't) _____________.　(4) My grandpa (can / can't) ___________.
(5) My grandma (can / can't) ________________.

Step 2　Rule-finding

Circle what shares in the above sentences (圈出上述句子中相似的地方).
Summarize the sentence patterns.

Sentence Patterns:

Step 3 Further Practicing

Judge whether each of the following sentences is correct in grammar. If it is correct, tick (√) it. If not, cross (×) it and write the correct sentence on the line.

(1) He can plays basketball. ( ) ____________________

(2) She can play the piano. ( ) ____________________

(3) Tom can does kung fu. ( ) ____________________

(4) Jenny can cooking. ( ) ____________________

教学时长: 15 mins

教学建议:

语法部分主要用于练习，旨在巩固词汇和语法知识。学生自行在课前或课后完成，教师批改。课堂上，教师带领学生总结存在的问题和解决办法。

1. 自我检测环节。

该活动要求学生完成句子，表达自己及家人是否能做词汇表里的活动。检测学生对句型 "What can you / he / she do?" 以及 "can" 的肯定式和否定式的应用。

2. 总结规则环节。

教师引导学生圈出第一个活动中5个句子中相同的词，可做一两个示范。教师引导学生关注重点句型: What can you do? / I can... / I can't...

3. 巩固练习环节。

教师引导学生发现题目中的语法错误，巩固学生对 "can" 的运用，比如 "can" 没有人称变化，其后跟动词原形。

参考答案:

(1) He can plays basketball. (×) He can play basketball

(2) She can play the piano. (√)

(3) Tom can does kung fu. (×) Tom can do kung fu.

(4) Jenny can cooking. (×) Jenny can cook.

思维试纸:

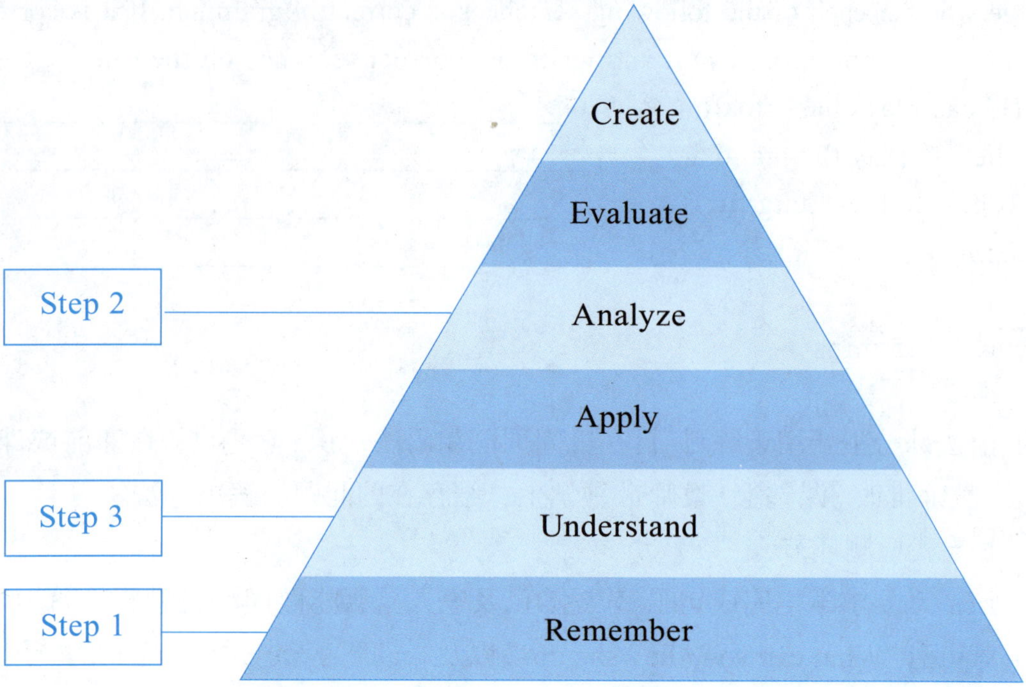
Create
Evaluate
Step 2
Analyze
Apply
Step 3
Understand
Step 1
Remember

Unit 5　There Is a Big Bed

单元导览

单元话题：房间物品

素材来源：PEP 5A Unit 5 There Is a Big Bed

教学时长：3 hrs

教学目标：

By the end of the lessons, students will be able to

语言目标：

1. read and **recognize** the meaning, sound and form of the words (bike, clock, plant, photo and water bottle) and **describe** their positions by associating expressions about direction (beside, in front of, behind, above, between);

2. **understand** conversations in the textbook, **describe** things in the room by using sentence structure (there be...), **describe** the location of the item accurately, **introduce** the room layout, and skillfully use the words and sentences in the situation.

非语言目标：

1. **introduce** their own rooms with confidence in front of the class;

2. cooperate with group members to **design** their rooms;

3. cultivate awareness of loving their rooms as part of emotional education;

4. strengthen their higher order thinking skills: **analyzing**, **evaluating** and **creating**.

融思设计

Part One　Listening and Speaking

教学素材: Part B Let's Talk

教学步骤:

Step 1　Preparation before Listening

1. **Guess** a riddle.

You can clean me up, but you can't move me.

You can dress me up, and you can live in me.

What am I?

2. **Brainstorm**: What there is / are in a living room.

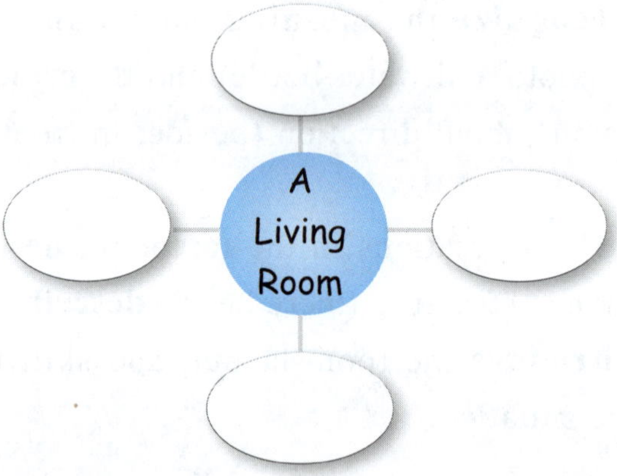

Step 2　Listening Comprehension

1. Listen and **tick** what room it is.

☐ bedroom　☐ study　☐ living room　☐ kitchen

2. Listen and **tick** what there are in the room.

☐ some pictures　☐ some plants　☐ some toys　☐ some flowers

Step 3 Preparation before Speaking

Fill in the blanks based on the picture in the textbook.

	Objects in the Living Room
pictures	There are some ________; they are ________ the TV.
plants	There are some ________; they are ________ the window.
books	There are some ________; they are ________ the bookshelf.
fish	There are some ________; they are ________ the fish bowl.
dogs	There are two ________. The yellow dog is ________ the table, and the black dog is ________ the table.
…	…

Step 4 Speaking and Sharing

1. Wu Yifan's family is moving into a new house. Can you **design** a bedroom for him?

Wu Yifan's Bedroom

2. **Describe** what there is / are in your bedroom, **evaluate** your designs and decide on the best design in your group.

Language Kit

There is a TV in the front of the living room.

There are some / many…

in / on / under / above / in front of / beside / between…

3. **Share** the best design of your group to the class.

Hello, everyone! We are glad to introduce our group's best design for Wu Yifan's bedroom. There is / are…

教学时长: 1.5 hrs

教学建议:

1. 听力准备环节。

(1) 猜谜: 教师可以先带领学生复习有关房间的相关词汇, 再呈现谜语, 学生根据描述猜测。如果学生猜测有困难, 教师还可以缩小猜测范围, 提供线索, 比如这个物品名称是几个字母组成的单词。

(2) 教师引导学生以头脑风暴形式描述自己卧室里有什么物品, 并呈现在气泡图里。

2. 听力理解环节。

(1) 教师引导学生根据录音信息辨别房间类型: 这是一间客厅。

(2) 教师播放录音, 学生听录音并勾出房间物品。教师播放一遍对话录音, 学生完成练习。教师根据学生完成情况可再播放一遍, 并进行校对。

There are pictures and plants.

3. 表达准备环节。

教师引导学生基于听力理解和教材的配图完成图表, 呈现房间里的物品及其位置。教师可以借机复习部分学生已知的方位介词, 比如in, on, under等, 注意辅助学生区别on和above。

4. 表达与分享环节。

（1）学生根据卧室实际面积、实际需要以及喜好完成卧室的设计图，包括摆设的物品、家具及其所在位置。教师可以布置学生在课前完成设计图并带到教室作为活动资源。

（2）教师将学生分成4~5人小组，小组成员拿出卧室设计图并用"There is / are..."句型和方位介词描述介绍。小组成员对设计进行互评并选定最好的卧室设计图。教师可以先引导学生在互评时给出具体的理由，丰富学生的语言表达。

（3）小组向全班轮流呈现介绍各组最好的卧室设计图。教师可以适时点评。

参考答案：

Hello, everyone! We are glad to introduce our group's best design for Wu Yifan's bedroom. There is a small bed on the left. There is a table and a chair beside the bed. And there are many books on the table, such as Chinese books, English books, story books and so on. On the walls there are some photos of Wu Yifan and his family. What a beautiful bedroom!

思维试纸：

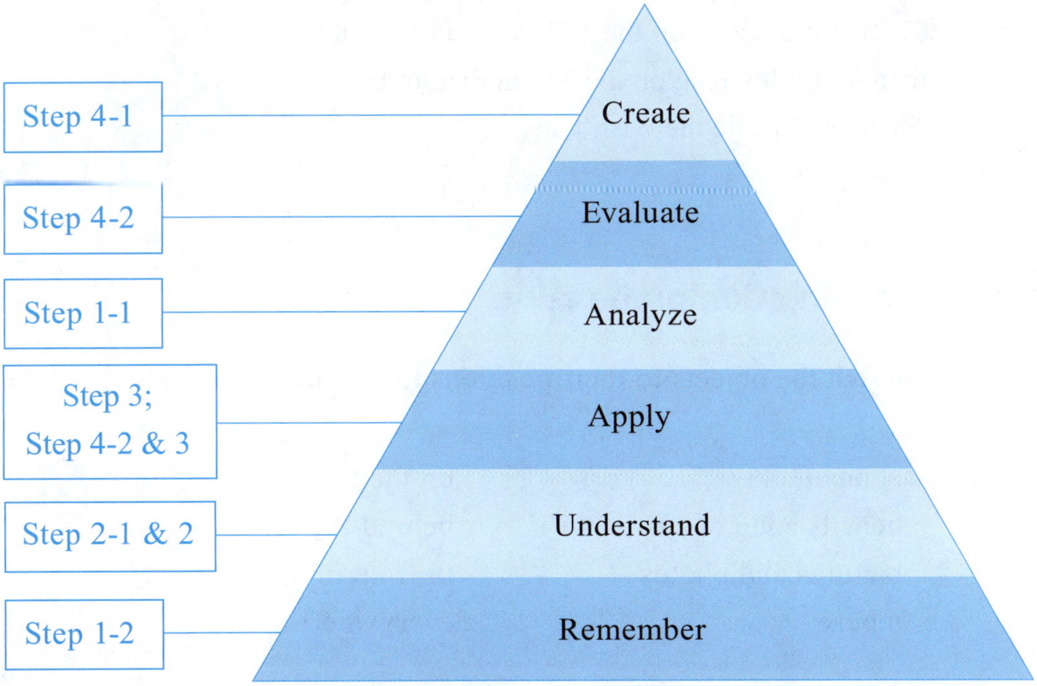

Part Two Reading and Writing

教学素材: Part B Read and Write

教学步骤:

Step 1 Preparation for Reading

What's different?

Contrast and describe the differences between Picture A and Picture B.

A

B

Language Kit

There are 2 books on the bed in Picture A but there is a schoolbag on the bed in Picture B.

There is... while there isn't any...

Step 2 Reading Comprehension

1. Skim to **match** the objects to their positions in Mr. Jones' room.

computer	on the floor
pencils and crayons	behind the computer
pictures and photos	in front of the mouse
mouse	everywhere

2. **Think about** why Mr. Jones ask for help and how Robin would help him. Put down your ideas in the two charts.

Step 3 Preparation before Writing

Mr. Jones left the messy room. Now Robin will help Mr. Jones to **relocate** the objects in the room to make it clean and tidy. Can you help him?

Objects	Positions Before	Positions Now
pencils and crayons		
pictures and photos		
mouse		

Step 4 Writing and Sharing

Write an email to Mr. Jones to tell him the room is clean and tidy now, and describe the room to him.

Dear Mr. Jones,

I am Robin the robot. Your room is ________________ now.

____

____

____

____

____

教学时长：1 hr

教学建议：

1. 读前准备环节。

读前活动类似大家来找茬游戏，要求学生通过比较两幅相似的房间的图片，找出其中的不同之处。教师引导学生观察、对比图片，调取自身储备的有关知识来找出两个房间的不同之处，包括物品名称、物品数量、物品位置等。教师可以根据学生水平提供描述两者不同之处的句式。

2. 阅读理解环节。

（1）学生运用跳读技巧找出Mr. Jones房间物品及其在房间的位置。

computer	on the floor
pencils and crayons	behind the computer
pictures and photos	in front of the mouse
mouse	everywhere

（2）教师引导学生思考文末Mr. Jones 向Robin求救的理由以及Robin可以给予Mr. Jones 哪些帮助。

3. 写作准备环节。

教师设置活动情境：Robin 收到邮件后决定帮助Mr. Jones整理房间物品，使之井然有序。教师请学生和Robin一起来做，并通过图表形式将物品的位置进行调整，比如将铅笔从地板上放入文具袋，蜡笔放入蜡笔盒，照片放入相册，图片放入文件夹等。教师还可以引导学生思考如何更好地收纳家里的物品。

4. 写作与分享环节。

教师引导学生帮助Robin给Mr. Jones写一封邮件，告诉他房间物品现在的摆放收纳情况。

参考答案：

Dear Mr. Jones,

I am Robin the robot. Your room is clean and tidy now. The pencils are in the pencil case. The crayons are in the red box on the table. The photos are in the photo album in the drawer of the table. And the pictures are all in the left drawer of the table. Guess where the mouse is now? I throw it out of the window! Don't worry about it! Now you can come back home.

Yours,

Robin

思维试纸:

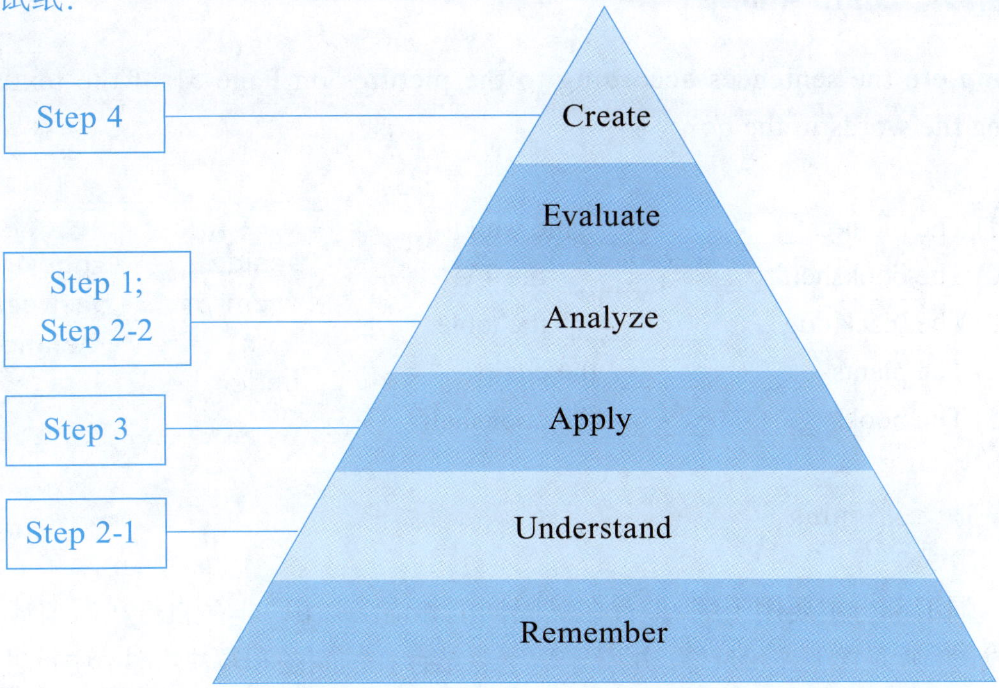

Part Three Vocabulary

教学素材: bike, clock, plants, photos, water bottle, window, books, in front of, beside, above, between, behind

教学步骤:

Step 1 Word Searching

Circle the 7 words of the objects in the room. The first one has been done for you.

b	a	y	m	i	n	t	o	n	d
w	w	i	n	d	o	w	l	z	i
c	h	u	p	t	a	h	a	l	f
p	e	c	h	y	b	o	o	k	s
l	z	l	o	a	t	r	a	k	e
a	n	o	t	b	o	t	t	l	e
n	c	c	o	i	v	e	h	u	e
t	j	k	s	k	e	p	t	l	n
s	r	a	b	i	k	e	r	d	t

Step 2　Blank-filling

Complete the sentences according to the pictures on Page 51 of the textbook, using the words in the box.

(1) The pictures _______ _______ the wall.
(2) The bookshelf _______ _______ the TV.
(3) The black dog _______ _______ the table.
(4) The plants _______ _______ the chairs.
(5) The books _______ _______ the bookshelf.

beside　above
in front of　between
on　behind
under

教学时长: 15 mins

教学建议:

词汇部分主要用于练习，旨在巩固词汇和语法知识。学生自行在课前或课后完成，教师课堂上评价反馈，并引导学生总结存在的问题和解决办法，注重巩固学生对本单元重点单词词性、词义的理解。

1. Step 1为圈词活动，由学生自行完成，教师引导学生从所给字母图表中圈出七个本单元所学的单词。

b	a	y	m	i	n	t	o	n	d
w	w	i	n	d	o	w	l	z	i
c	h	u	p	t	a	h	a	l	f
p	e	c	h	y	b	o	o	k	s
l	z	l	o	a	t	r	a	k	e
a	n	o	t	b	o	t	t	l	e
n	c	c	o	i	v	e	h	u	e
t	j	k	s	k	e	p	t	l	n
s	r	a	b	i	k	e	r	d	t

2. Step 2由学生根据教材51页图片上的物品及其位置完成句子。

(1) The pictures are on the wall.
(2) The bookshelf is beside the TV.
(3) The black dog is on the table.
(4) The plants are in front of the chairs.
(5) The books are on the bookshelf.

思维试纸:

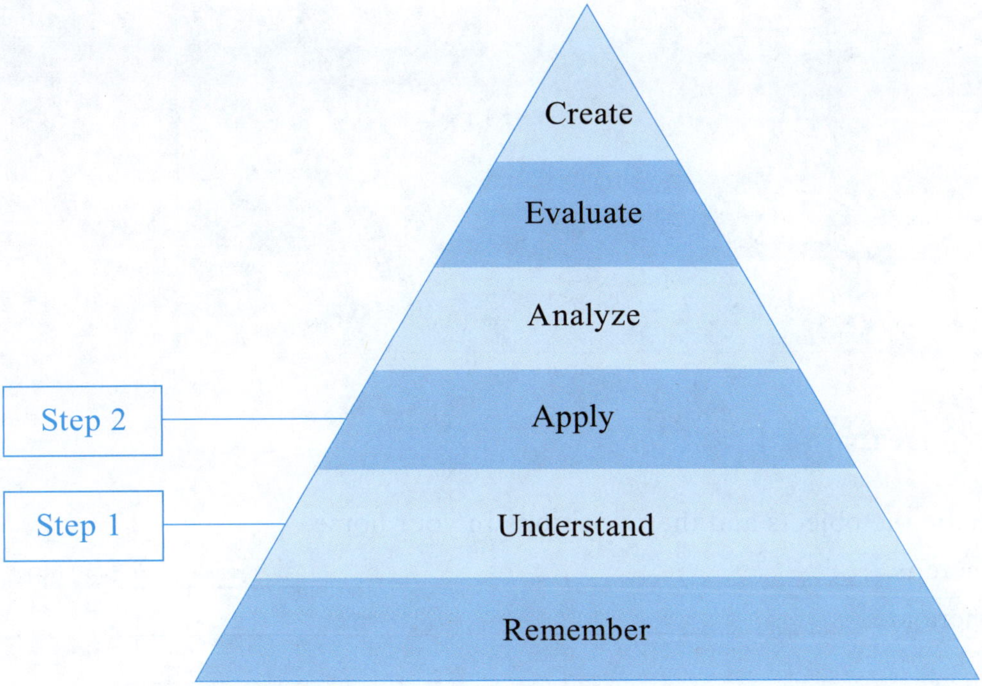

Part Four Grammar

教学素材: What is in the room? / It's... / There is...

Where is the...? / It's...

教学步骤:

Step 1 Self-checking

Complete the sentences with proper words.

(1) There ___________ a book on my table.

There ___________ some books on my table.

(2) There is a ___________ in my schoolbag.

There are some ___________ in my schoolbag.

Step 2 Rule-finding

1. **Circle** what shares in the above sentences.

2. **Summarize** the sentence patterns.

Step 3　Further Practicing

Describe the objects and their positions in your home.

(1) There is ______________________________.

(2) There are ______________________________.

(3) ______________________________

(4) ______________________________

(5) ______________________________

My Home

教学时长: 15 mins

教学建议:

语法部分主要用于练习，旨在巩固词汇和语法知识。学生自行在课前或课后完成，教师批改。课堂上，教师带领学生总结存在的问题和解决办法。

1. 自我检测环节。

该活动主要检测学生对“There be...”句型中“is”和“are”的正确运用。学生可以根据后面所跟名词的单复数来确定是用“is”还是“are”。

(1) There is a book on my table.

There are some books on my table.

(2) There is a ruler in my schoolbag.

There are some pens in my schoolbag.

2. 总结规则环节。

教师引导学生观察例句，圈出句子中共同的“there is / are”部分，引导学生有意识地学习句型“There is / are...”，尤其注意句中单复数的变化。

3. 巩固练习环节。

学生自主运用所学句型描述自己卧室里的物品及其位置。教师也可要求学生在句子旁边画出自家房屋结构和布局草图，以检测学生语言描述是否准确。

参考答案：

This is my home. There are 6 rooms, a living room, a kitchen, a bathroom, a study and 2 bedrooms. Here is my bedroom. There is a small blue bed on the left. There is a table and a chair beside the bed. On the table, there is a plant and my books. I often do my homework at the table. On the right of the room, there is a wardrobe. And there are some photos on the walls. I love my bedroom.

思维试纸：

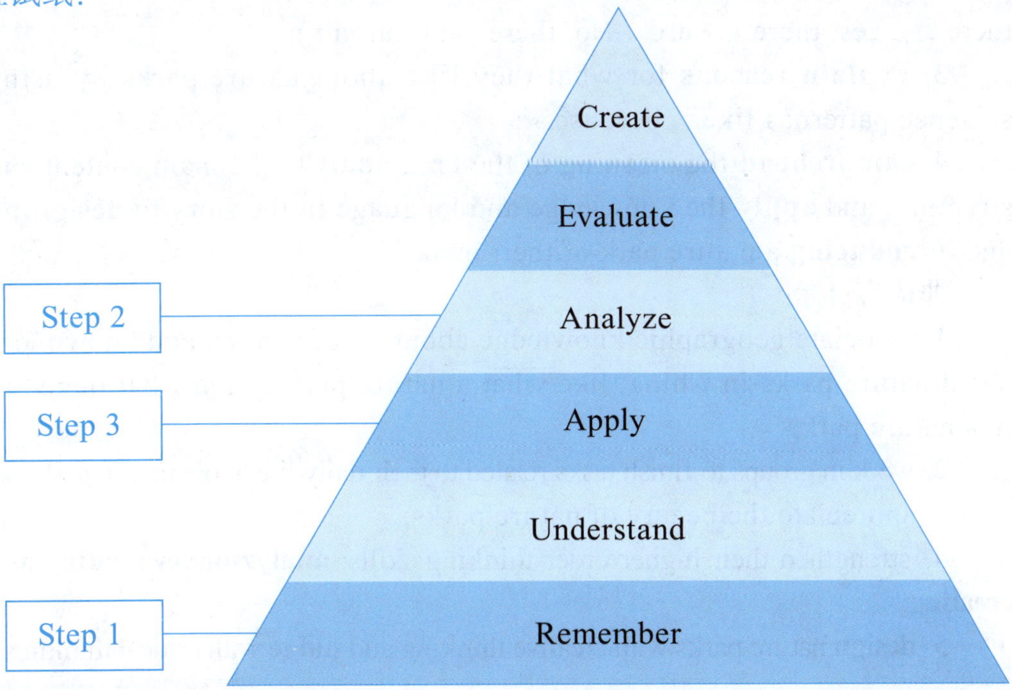

Unit 6 In a Nature Park

单元导览

单元话题: 自然地理
素材来源: PEP 5A Unit 6 In a Nature Park
教学时长: 3 hrs
教学目标:

By the end of the lessons, students will be able to

语言目标:

1. **name** the things in a nature park (forest, mountain, hill, lake, river, tree, house, building, bridge) in English and describe their features;

2. **understand** conversations in the textbook and talk about nature parks in China by using sentence patterns (There is / are... / Is / Are there... / Yes, there is / are. / No, there isn't / aren't.);

3. **explain** reasons for what they like about nature parks by using sentence pattern: I like... because...;

4. **comprehend** the meaning of the text, **analyze** the main content and structure, and **apply** the knowledge and language in the story to **designing** and **introducing** a nature park of their own.

非语言目标:

1. associate geographic knowledge about nature parks, and know more about nature parks in China, like what a nature park is and what there are in a nature park;

2. work in groups to finish tasks related to their daily life about nature parks;

3. appreciate the beauty of nature parks;

4. strengthen their higher order thinking skills: **analyzing**, **evaluating** and **creating**;

5. **design** nature parks with creative thinking and **judge** with critical thinking.

融思设计

Part One Listening and Speaking

教学素材: Part A & Part B Let's Talk
教学步骤:

Step 1 Preparation before Listening

1. **Tick** the nature park from the following three pictures.

A

B

C

2. **List** the differences in the three kinds of parks.

Step 2 Listening Comprehension

1. Listen and **decide** whether the statements are True or False.

Part A Let's Talk

(1) There is a river in the forest. ( )

(2) There is a lake and some boats in the forest. ( )

Part B Let's Talk

(3) There are many people in the nature park. ( )

(4) There are some animals in the nature park. ( )

(5) There are many tall buildings in the nature park. ( )

2. **Find out** what there is / are in a nature park.

There is / are { } in a nature park.

Step 3 Preparation before Speaking

Prepare a picture of your favorite nature park, and **mark** what there is / are in the nature park.

My Favorite Nature Park

Step 4 Speaking and Sharing

1. Work in pairs to **complete** a picture of a nature park by asking questions.

A Nature Park

A

B

Language Kit

Is there a... in the nature park?

Are there... in the nature park?

Where is the...?

It is beside / near / in front of the...

2. **Decide** if the following things are a part of a nature park. Share your ideas in your group and tell why or why not.

wild animals	rivers	mountains	tents
merry-go-round	garbage	playground	lakes
roller-coaster	trees	grassland	

Language Kit

I think... is / are a part of a nature park because...

I don't think... is / are a part of a nature park because...

教学时长: 1.5 hrs

教学建议:

1. 听力准备环节。

（1）学生从三幅图片中选出自然公园图。教师可以引导学生对比三幅图片，思考自然公园、城市公园和游乐园的区别。

（2）教师引导学生列举自然公园、城市公园和游乐园三者之间的差别。教师可以根据学生需要补充相关词汇和句型。

2. 听力理解环节。

该活动作为对话讲解的补充练习，教师可把Part A和Part B两篇对话内容结合起来教学。教师播放对话录音，学生完成练习。教师根据学生完成情况可再播放一遍，并进行校对。

（1）学生听录音，判断正误。第一部分为“Part A Let's Talk”的内容，第二部分为“Part B Let's Talk”的内容。句子内容主要为森林和自然公园里的自然景观。

参考答案：

Part A: F; T

Part B: F; T; F

（2）学生根据对话内容总结自然公园里有哪些自然景观。教师可以引导学生回忆游览过的自然公园，包括自然公园的名称、地理位置、主要景观等。教师可以根据学生的回答适当补充相关词汇和表达法，比如山脉的英文表达，可以是“xx mountain”，也可以是“Mount xx”。

There is a lake and some boats in the forest.

There are some animals in the nature park.

There are ducks and rabbits.

3. 表达准备环节。

教师安排学生在学完两篇对话后完成。学生在课前准备一张自己喜欢的自然公园图片，也可以由学生自己绘画，并在图片上标注公园里的自然景观名称，比如山脉名、湖泊名等。

4. 表达与分享环节。

（1）学生两人一组，教师将A、B版不完整的自然公园图片分别发给两个学生。学生运用“Is there a... in the nature park? / Are there... in the nature park? / Where is the...? / It is beside / near / in front of the...”等句型问答，获取信息，完成自己的自然公园图片。

（2）学生根据自己的认知，判断野生动物（wild animals）、垃圾（garbage）、湖泊（lakes）、过山车（roller coaster）、旋转木马（merry-go-round）等是否是属于自然公园的一部分。教师引导学生思考人类应如何保护自然公园，提高学生的环保意识。

参考答案：

I think trees, mountains, lakes... are a part of a nature park because they are natural scenes and they help to protect nature. I don't think garbage is a part of a nature park because it is waste material, such as paper, plastic bags, and it pollutes and destroys the nature. I don't think merry-go-round and roller coaster are a part of a nature park because they are facilities in amusement parks for fun and excitement.

思维试纸:

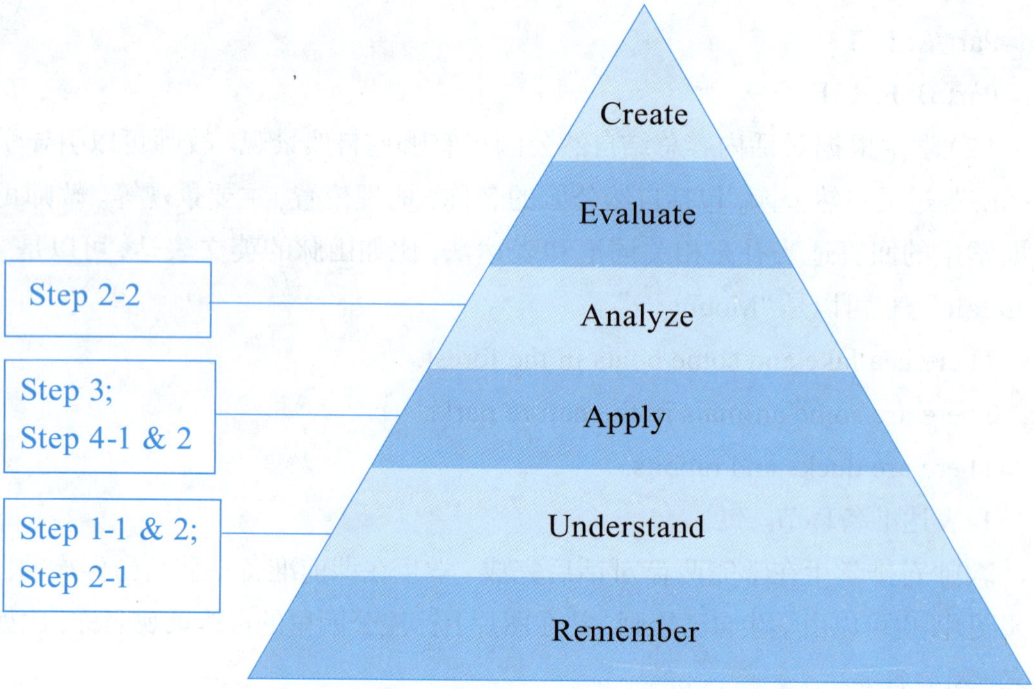

Part Two　Reading and Writing

教学素材: Part B Read and Write

教学步骤:

Step 1　Preparation for Reading

Predict where Robin is and what he is looking at.

Who?　Robin

Where? ____________________

What? ____________________

Step 2 Reading Comprehension

1. **List** what Robin sees in the nature park.

____

____

____

____

2. **Find out** the locations of what there is / are in the nature park.

(1) There is ______________ the village.
(2) There is ______________ Mr. Jones' house.
(3) There are ______________ the lake.
(4) There is a high ______________ the park.
(5) There is ______________ the mountain.

Step 3 Preparation before Writing

List what you would like to see in a nature park and **design** a nature park.
A group of American visitors are going sightseeing in China. Recommend them a Chinese nature park by drawing a picture of it.

Step 4 Writing and Sharing

1. Write to **describe** what there is / are in the nature park you recommend and the locations.

> The nature park is ____________________. There is / are ________________ in the nature park. ____________________ the nature park, there is / are ____________________________ ____.

2. **Find** your "friend": Ask your group members if they and you have the same things in your nature parks. If you have more than 3 things in common, you are "friends".

> — What is / are there in your nature park?
> — There is / are ___________ in my nature park.

教学时长: 1 hr

教学建议:

1. 读前准备环节。

(1) 教师引导学生根据图片猜测Robin现在哪里，在看什么。学生调取自身储备知识，补充自然地理知识，回想自然公园相关单词，丰富自然公园相关词汇。

(2) 教师根据学生已有的自然地理知识，预测Robin看到的自然公园是什么样子的，里面有什么。

2. 阅读理解环节。

(1) 学生阅读文本，勾画自然公园关键词，并填入表格。教师可以引导学生对比自己的预测，找出相同和不同之处。

A high mountain, a small village, a lake, many ducks.

(2) 教师引导学生根据文本信息，找出自然公园里各处景观的位置并填空。

There is a lake near the village.

There is a nature park near Mr. Jones' house.

There are many ducks on the lake.

There is a high mountain in the park.

There is a small village in front of the mountain.

3. 写作准备环节。

学生在课堂上列举自己最喜欢的自然公园里的景观并运用沙盘或图画形式设计一个自然公园。

4. 写作与分享环节。

(1) 学生描述自己设计的自然公园模型内容及其相应的地理位置。

(2) 学生通过"找朋友"活动相互询问各自设计的自然公园里有什么，如果有三种或以上相同的景观或物品，这两个同学就交友成功，并大声说"Bingo"。

参考答案：

There is a beautiful nature park… in… In the park, there is a river. There is a bridge over the river. There aren't any tall buildings in the park. But there are many wild animals, such as rabbits, butterflies, birds and so on in the nature park. There are many trees beside the river. The water is clean, and the air is fresh. The nature park is so nice. I like it very much!

思维试纸：

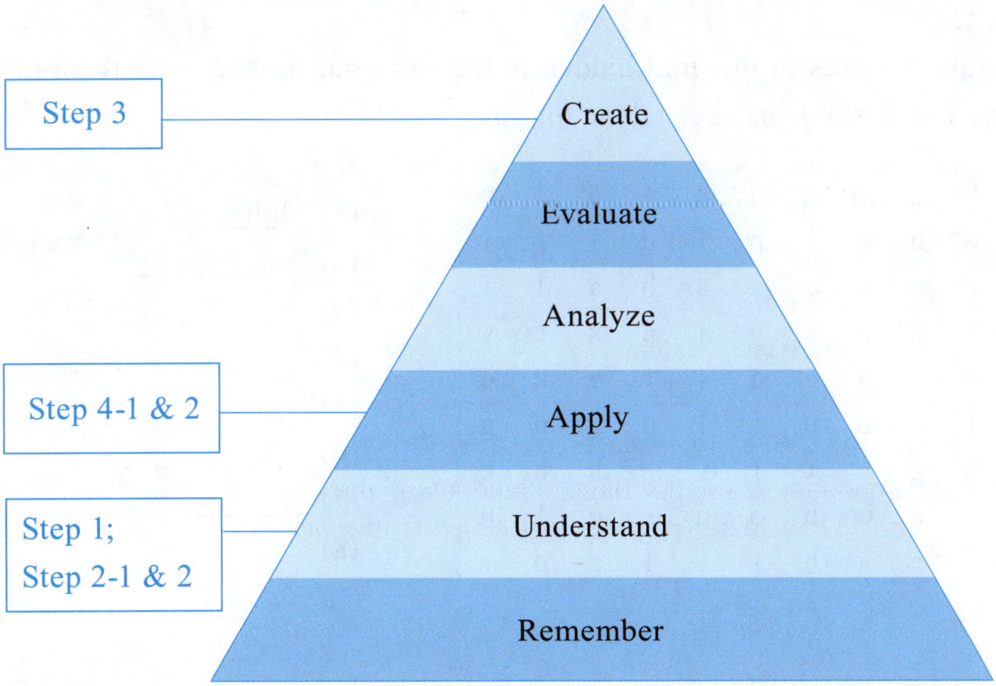

Part Three　Vocabulary

教学素材：forest, mountain, hill, lake, river, tree, house, building, bridge, 表颜色的词汇及表形状的形容词（big, small, long, high, etc.）

教学步骤：

Step 1　Self-checking

Write down what there is / are in a nature park in the blanks.

____

____

____

____

____

Step 2　Word Searching

Circle the 8 words in this unit hidden in the word puzzle and write them in the blanks. The first one has been done for you.

b	a	m	o	u	n	t	a	i	n
w	h	e	l	p	f	u	l	z	i
c	b	u	e	t	a	h	a	l	f
f	r	n	s	y	l	a	k	e	y
o	i	g	e	a	t	r	a	k	e
r	d	b	u	i	l	d	i	n	g
e	g	e	t	i	v	e	h	u	e
s	e	w	h	o	u	s	e	l	n
t	r	a	h	i	l	l	r	d	t

(1) hill

(2) ______________

(3) ______________

(4) ______________

(5) ______________

(6) ______________

(7) ______________

(8) ______________

教学时长: 15 mins

教学建议:

词汇部分主要用于练习，旨在巩固词汇和语法知识。学生自行在课前或课后完成，教师批改。课堂上，教师带领学生总结存在的问题和解决办法，注重巩固学生对本单元重点单词词性、词义的理解。教师可以根据学生水平适当拓展相关新词汇或者复习旧词汇，比如表颜色的单词和表形状的形容词。

1. Step 1: 学生在图表空白处填写自然公园里有什么。本活动答案不唯一，教师可以引导学生尽可能多地写出与自然公园相关的单词，并根据学生水平适当拓展。

2. Step 2: 学生在字母迷宫图中圈出与自然公园相关的词汇，并将单词写在横线上。

b	a	m	o	u	n	t	a	i	n
w	h	e	l	p	f	u	l	z	i
c	b	u	e	t	a	h	a	l	f
f	r	n	s	y	l	a	k	e	y
o	i	g	e	a	t	r	a	k	e
r	d	b	u	i	l	d	i	n	g
e	g	e	t	i	v	e	h	u	e
s	e	w	h	o	u	s	e	l	n
t	r	a	h	i	l	l	r	d	t

思维试纸:

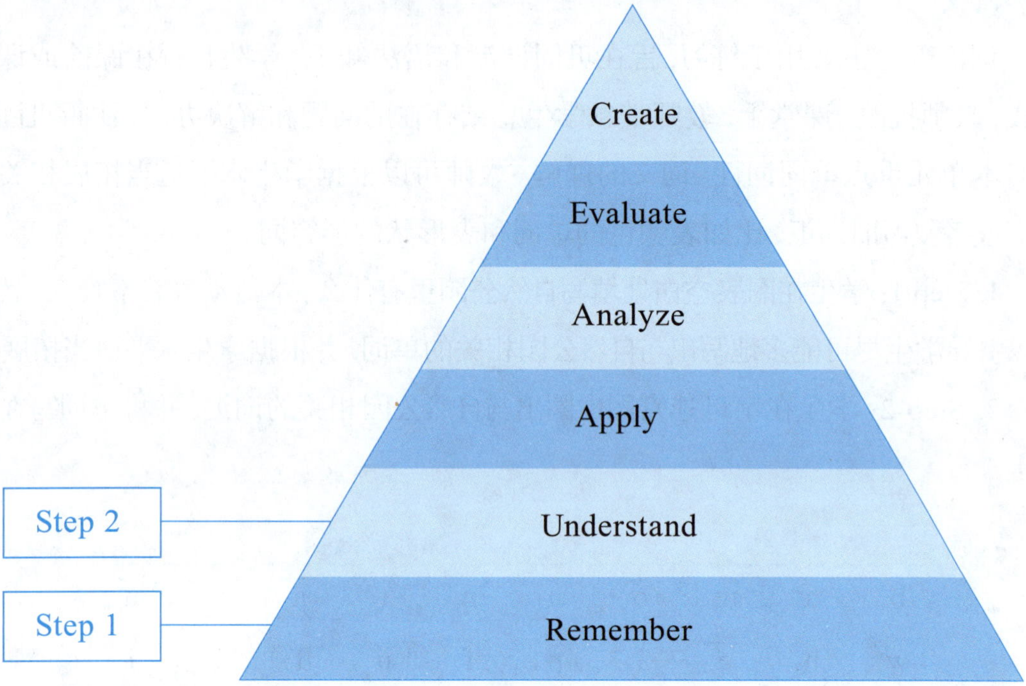

Part Four Grammar

教学素材: There is / are…

Is there a…? / Yes, there is. / No, there isn't.

Are there some…? / Yes, there are. / No, there aren't.

教学步骤:

Step 1 Self-checking

Fill in the blanks to complete the conversation in pairs and draw a picture of a nature park based on the conversation.

— Is there a high ______________ in the nature park?
— Yes, there is.
— ________________ wild animals in it?
— Yes, there are. There are ____________________.
— ____?
— Yes, there is, and there is a bridge on it.
— Are there any people in the nature park?
— ____________________. It is very quiet.

Step 2 Rule-finding

Circle what shares in the above sentences.

Summarize the sentence patterns and the usage of them.

Step 3 Further Practicing

1. Here are some sentences about your hometown Chongqing. **Judge** whether the following sentences are correct in grammar. If it is correct, tick it. If not, cross it and correct the mistake.

(1) There are a river in Chongqing. (　　)
(2) There is many bridges in Chongqing. (　　)
(3) — Are there any boats on the river? (　　)
　— Yes, there is. (　　)
(4) Is there a tall mountain in Chongqing? (　　)
(5) Is there trees in the mountain? (　　)
(6) On front of the mountain, there is a village. (　　)
(7) There are many places of interest in Chongqing. (　　)
(8) — Are there any tall buildings in Chongqing? (　　)
　— Yes, there aren't. (　　)

2. A 10-year-old American boy would like to visit some cities in China. **Write** a short paragraph to recommend Chongqing to him.

Chongqing is my hometown. There…______________________
____
____
____
____
____
____

教学时长: 15 mins

教学建议:

语法部分主要用于练习，旨在巩固词汇和语法知识。学生自行在课前或课后完成，教师批改反馈。课堂上，教师带领学生总结存在的问题和解决办法。

1. 自我检测环节。

该部分要求学生两人一组，小组根据提示完成关于自然公园的对话，然后根据对话内容绘制一幅自然公园图画。教师可以引导学生注意“high mountain”词组的搭配。完整的对话示范如下：

—Is there a high mountain in the nature park?

—Yes, there is.

—Are there wild animals in it?

—Yes, there are. There are tigers and elephants.

—Is there a river in it?

—Yes, there is, and there is a bridge on it.

—Are there any people in the nature park?

—No, there aren't. It is very quiet.

2. 总结规则环节。

教师引导学生观察自我检测环节中的句子，圈出句子中共同的部分，并总结归纳主要句型，包括“there be”句型的单复数、一般疑问句及其肯定和否定回答形式，鼓励学生分享阐述如何使用“there be”句型。学生可以使用汉语阐述。

3. 巩固练习环节。

（1）教师引导学生观察分析所给句子，运用“there be”句型语法知识判断句子正误，并修改错误句子。

（2）教师介绍活动情境：一位10岁的美国小男孩想要来中国旅游，要求学生运用所给句子完成一篇关于家乡重庆的短文写作，向小男孩推荐家乡重庆。学生可以根据自己的了解和想法，补充拓展更多关于重庆特色的描述，比如：There are many places of interest. There are two rivers in Chongqing. One is the Yangtze River and the other is the Jialing River. Chongqing is known as the Mountainous City. There are many high mountains, such as…

判断正误参考答案：

（1）There are a river in Chongqing. (×) — There is a river in Chongqing.

（2）There is many bridges in Chongqing. (×) — There are many bridges in Chongqing.

(3) —Are there any boats on the river? (√)

—Yes, there is. (×) — Yes, there are.

(4) Is there a tall mountain in Chongqing? (×) — Is there a high mountain in Chongqing?

(5) Is there trees in the mountain? (×) — Are there trees in the mountain?

(6) On front of the mountain, there is a village. (×) — In front of the mountain, there is a village.

(7) There are many places of interest in Chongqing. (√)

(8) — Are there any tall buildings in Chongqing? (√)

— Yes, there aren't. (×) — Yes, there are.

思维试纸:

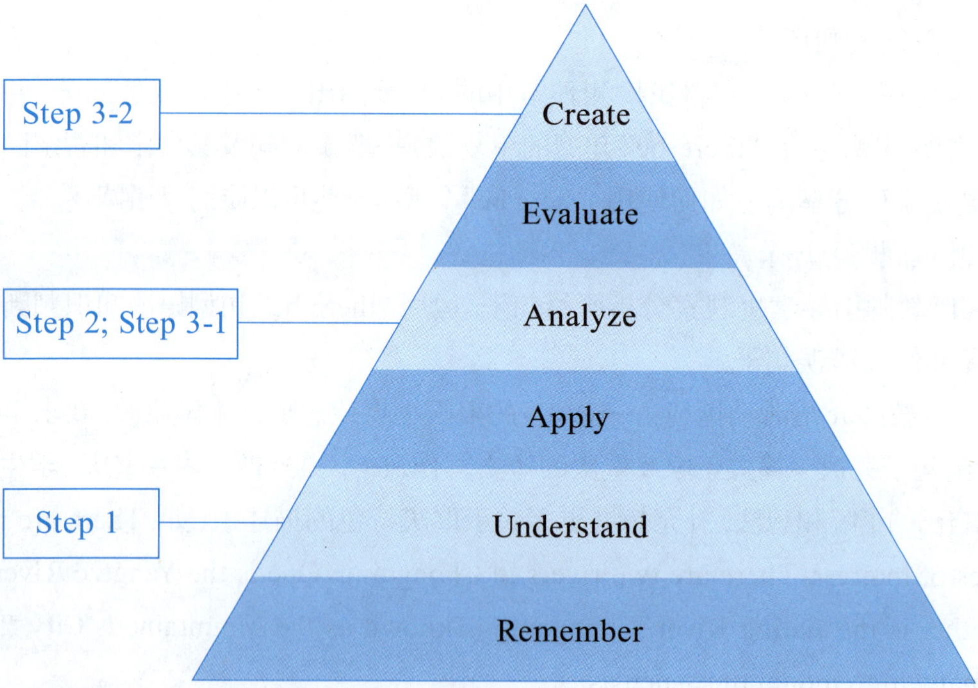

5B

Unit 1 My Day

单元导览

单元话题：我的一天
素材来源：PEP 5A Unit 1 My Day
教学时长：3 hrs
教学目标：

By the end of the lesson, students will be able to

语言目标：

1. **comprehend** the listening text by differentiating the activities of fun and the ones of hard work, by **identifying** the logical relationships with the word "so" and "but";

2. **discuss** what they normally do on Saturdays / Sundays in the conversation;

3. read and **understand** the text of *Robin's Play*, **sequence** Robinson's daily activities, **find out** expressions **indicating** time order and **compare** the frequency of different activities;

4. observe, **organize** and write down their daily activities in a letter;

5. **comprehend** and **remember** phrases related to daily activities (do morning exercises, eat breakfast, have… class, play sports, eat dinner, clean one's room, go for a walk, go shopping and take a dancing class) by **matching** the meaning and the form, and by **categorizing** them;

6. **understand** and **apply** frequency adverbs (sometimes, usually, often, always) to **making** sentences in the new context.

非语言目标：

1. enhance thinking skills: **applying**, **classifying**, **sequencing**,

comparing, **contrasting**, **analyzing** cause and effect relationship to facilitate comprehension and memory;

2. work in groups to make a reasonable decision about fixing time with others, by **evaluating** different choices;

3. know the meaning of sharing, that is, to share something people do not know;

4. strengthen their empathy to others when making decisions.

融思设计

Part One Listening and Speaking

教学素材: Pat B Let's Talk

教学步骤:

Step 1 Listening Comprehension

1. Listen and **fill in** the blanks.

Mom __________ last night, —so→ Sara is __________ today.

2. Listen again, **tick** what Sarah does on the weekend and then fill in the blanks.

Sara often ______________. That sounds like a lot of fun.

But she is _____. She usually _______ and sometimes _______ on the weekend.

Step 2 Preparation before Speaking

Recall and **write** down what you normally do on Saturday.
Give 1–5 stars to what you do to show the importance (重要性).

Saturday		Importance
6:00–7:00	e.g. sleep	(☆☆☆☆☆)
7:00–8:00		
8:00–9:00		
9:00–10:00		
10:00–11:00		
11:00–12:00		
12:00–13:00		
13:00–14:00		
14:00–15:00		
16:00–17:00		

Step 3 Speaking and Sharing

You're going to have a picnic in the park on Saturday with three of your friends for three hours. You have different time schedules (时间表), and you need to **decide** when you can have the picnic together.

1. **Analyze** (分析) your own time schedule and think about when you will be free (有空的) and when you can change your plan (改变计划) to go to the picnic. Write

down "√" (can go for a picnic), "×" (cannot go for a picnic), or "?" (not sure 不确定) beside each time period in your time schedule. Write down your reasons.

Checklist	Reason
☐ ________	______________________________
☐ ________	______________________________
☐ ________	______________________________
☐ ________	______________________________
☐ ________	______________________________
☐ ________	______________________________

2. **Recommend** the proper time for your picnic and **explain** your reasons in group discussion. Fill in the form when sharing your ideas.

Names				
First Choice				
Second Choice				

You can **use** the sentence patterns below to discuss.

Language Kit

My first choice is…, because I am free from… to…

I (do sth.)… from… to…

My second choice is… because I (do sth.)… from… to… I can change (改变) it.

3. **Compare** (比较) your choices and circle the same choice(s). Then **decide** the time for picnic and **explain** why you make this decision.

Let’s go for a picnic

from

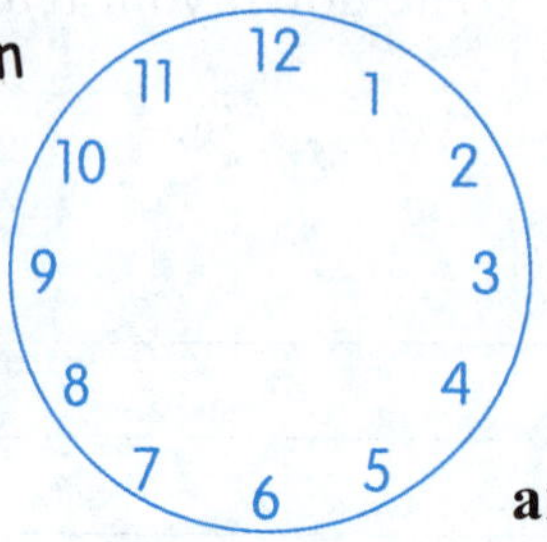

am / pm

to

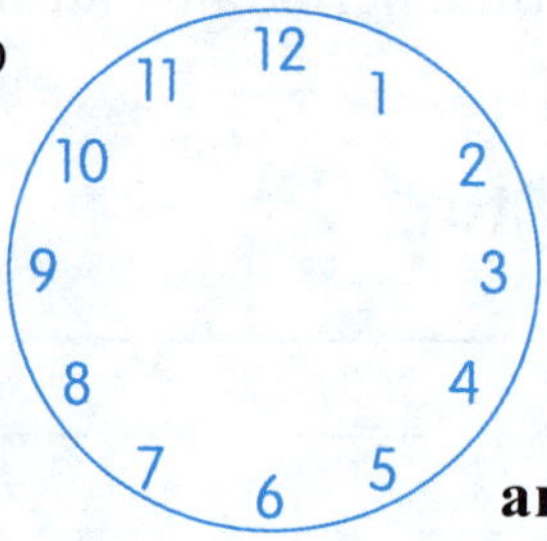

am / pm

Language Kit

We can go for a picnic from… to… because…

教学时长: 1.5 hrs

教学建议:

1. 听力理解环节。

(1) 学生听录音，根据听到的内容填空。

参考答案:

worked; shopping

(2) 学生再听一遍录音，选择Sarah周末要做的事情，并打钩，然后根据录音内容填空。在播放录音之前，教师可引导学生先观察图片，理解图片的意思，再进行听力练习。

参考答案:

watches TV and plays ping-pong with her father; hard-working; washes clothes; cooks dinner

2. 表达准备环节。

教师引导学生回顾并思考他们通常在星期六早上会做什么事情，然后让学生结合事情的重要性以及自己的真实情况填写表格。教师可引导学生先填写一栏作示范，然后让学生自行填写。

3. 表达与分享环节。

教师设置情境: 你将在星期六和三个朋友一起去野餐三个小时，但是每个人有不同的时间安排，你需要决定哪个时间段可以一起去野餐。

(1) 教师引导学生分析自己的时间表，看自己哪一个时间段是有空的，或者哪一个时间段可以为了野餐改变自己的计划。在可以去野餐的时间段前面打钩，不能去的打叉，不确定的时间段前面打问号，并说明理由。

(2) 学生为野餐推荐合适的时间，在小组内说明理由并填写表格。学生可以运用提供的句型模板进行表达和分享。教师可以先在一个小组内进行示范，先询问一个学生的时间选择，然后让他填写表格，之后再让学生自行选择并分享。

(3) 学生需要比较小组成员的选择并圈出相同的选择，然后决定去野餐的时间，并在钟面上画出选择的时间。教师可邀请学生在班上解释小组做这个决定的原因。

思维试纸：

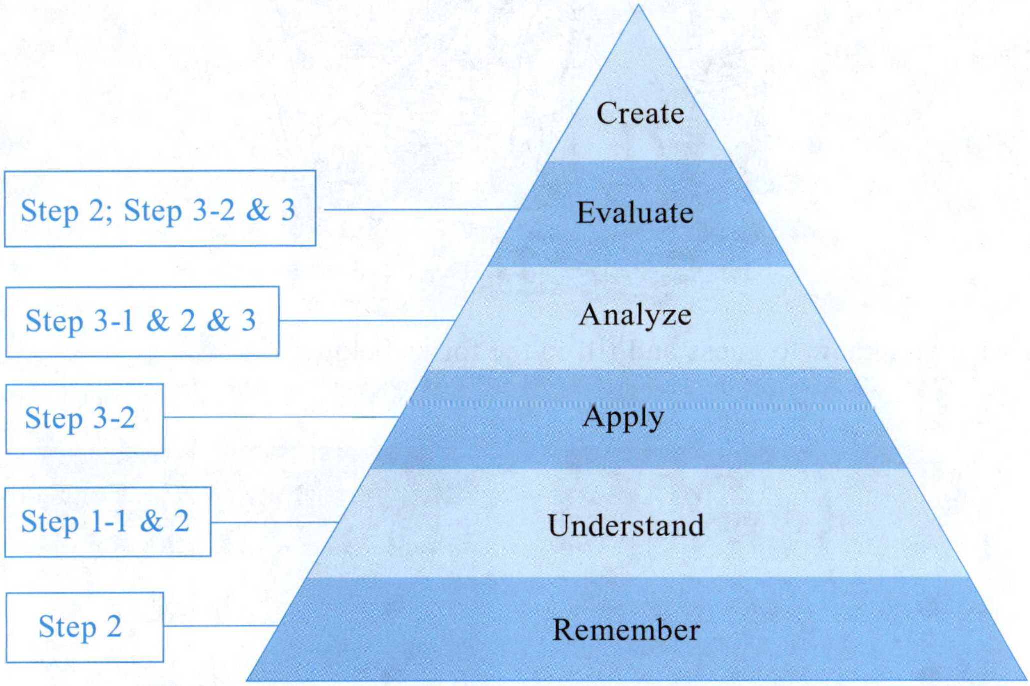

备注："思维试纸"将各教学活动中加粗的动词(思维技能)与思维层级匹配，使教学过程中的思维技能训练显性化。5B余下各单元的"思维试纸"不再一一备注。

Part Two Reading and Writing

教学素材: Part B Read and Write

教学步骤:

Step 1 Preparation before Reading

Imagine a person is living on the island based on the picture and **brainstorm** what he does in the morning and in the afternoon.

Use what you know to guess and fill in the forms below.

in the morning	in the afternoon
● ________	● ________
● ________	● ________
● ________	● ________

Step 2 Reading Comprehension

1. After you read Robin's play, **underline** what Robinson does in a day. **Match** them to your guessing, and tick the same ones in the above forms. Share in groups about how you find the answers.

Guessing right about

- ______________________________
- ______________________________
- ______________________________

2. **Match** and **fill in** the blanks with the activities of Robinson and **color** the column to **show** the frequencies. The more you color, the more frequent it is.

		0 (不涂) 100% (涂满)
always	________	
sometimes	________	
often	________	

Step 3 Preparation before Writing

1. **Recall** and **list** the activities you do every day (weekday and weekend), and **compare** them with Robinson's and write them down in the chart.

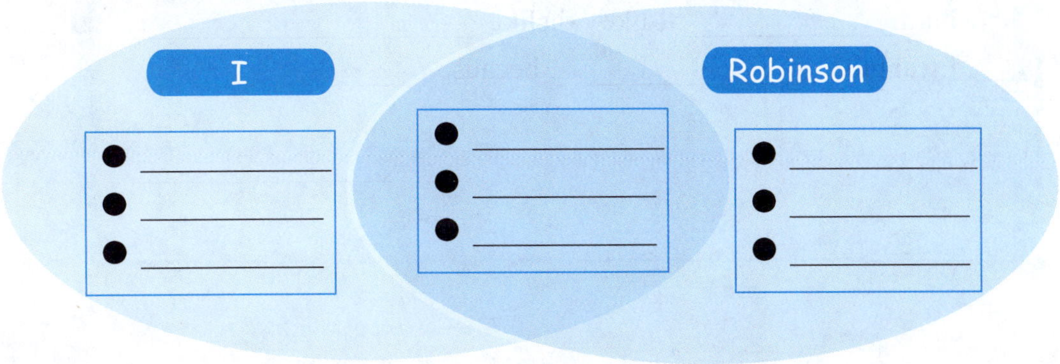

2. **Mark** your feelings when you do the activities by drawing the emojis (表情) beside them and **select** the ones you want to share with Robinson.

For example:

happy	sad	angry	excited	bored

3. Are you satisfied with your day? Do you want to change some activities? **Write down** your evaluation here and **explain** why.

I do not want to ______________________. I want to ________________________,
because ____.

Step 4 Writing and Sharing

1. What do you want to share with Robinson? **Write** about your day and your ideas.

Dear __________,

My name is ____________________________. I am a student.

We share a lot in common. We ____________________________.

We ______________________ ... I am ______________________.

But, I ________________________ I ________________________...

I am ______________. I like / dislike ______________________.

I want to ___________________, because ___________________ ...

Yours,

____

Language Kit

写信过程中，如果你想要知道对方的想法，可以使用"What about you?" "Do you like… / dislike…?"等问句。

2. Challenge yourself! Is there a person you like living in other countries? **Share** your life and ideas with him / her.

- Who is him / her? What does he / she do?
- Where is he / she living now?
- What does he / she often / sometimes / always do in his / her daily life?

What do you feel about his / her life?

教学时长：1 hr

教学建议：

1. 读前准备环节。

教师先让学生想象一个人生活在孤岛上，他在上午和下午会做什么，然后让学生根据自己的想象填写表格。

2. 阅读理解环节。

(1) 教师引导学生阅读完文本内容之后，和自己的猜想进行比较，将猜对部分的原文挑选出来，然后在小组内分享自己是如何快速找到答案的。这样可以帮助学生掌握更多的阅读技巧。

(2) 教师引导学生根据文本将答案填写在横线上，并在方框内涂色，以表示事情发生频率的高低。教师需要告诉学生，涂的面积越大，事情发生得越频繁。其目的在于帮助学生理解这三个频率副词的意思。

3. 写作准备环节。

（1）学生回忆并列出自己一天要做的事情，然后将自己的事情和Robinson的事情进行比较，并且思考自己的一天和Robinson一天所做的事情，哪些相同，哪些不同。教师提问：如果要给Robinson写信，你会分享哪些事情呢？

What things do you want to share with Robinson? The same things or different things?

（2）教师引导学生思考，除了分享做的事情，我们还会分享什么呢？（What else do you want to share?）学生如果没有讲到，教师可举例。（For example, share what you feel.）然后，教师引导学生在所写事情的旁边画出表情标记自己做这些活动时的心情。

（3）除了心情外，教师还要引导学生深入思考生活。教师询问学生对自己的一天是否满意，有没有想要改变的活动，然后让学生填写表格并解释原因。

4. 写作与分享环节。

（1）教师可以根据学生情况，让学生选择Robinson为写作对象，也可以让学生自行选择写作对象。如果写作对象不是Robinson，那么前面准备环节的比较对象要随之发生变化，学生需要自己思考对方每天会做些什么，比如爸爸、妈妈、自己的朋友。

（2）如果写作对象发生变化，教师可以考虑融合情感因素、文化因素，进一步升华该教学活动。

比如，写作对象是爸爸、妈妈，教师可以引导学生比较自己和父母的一天(包括晚上)，思考自己每天做这些事情的心情，也考虑父母的心情；思考自己想要改变的活动，也考虑父母想要自己做出哪些改变，从而激发学生的同理心。

（3）另外，假设是给美国、英国等其他国家的小朋友写信，尤其是在与其他国家本身有交流项目的情况下，教师可以让这封信变成真实的交际活动。如果是假设情境，那么教师需要补充这个小朋友一天的主要活动，比如一个英国小朋友的日常和一些有文化特色的活动。教师也可以引导学生询问“What do you _____ in the morning / in the afternoon / in the evening? Are you _____?”，激发学生对不同文化的好奇心。

（备注：写作对象的选择也取决于课时长度，Robison的用时最少，与阅读部分直接衔接即可；学生自己选择对象，如父母、朋友，相对比较熟悉，兴趣度更高，也能较快进行写作准备，但是教师要注意补充一些日常活动相关的词汇，比如：go to work, drive home, have lunch；而如果是教师预设外国小朋友或教师的情境，可能会涉及与新的文化活动相关的词汇，教师和学生都不熟悉，有一定难度，这种情况下可以直接进行Step 3的活动2和活动3，引导学生着重描述自己的情况，以及提问，在信中询问对方的情况。）

(4) 确定了写作对象之后，教师引导学生理解写信的目的，引出“分享”。教师引导学生进一步思考为什么要分享，让学生基于分享的理由来选择信中要写的事情。教师可以做如下提问：

Why do we want to write a letter about our day to our friend?

(Because we share similarities and differences / Because we share same or different feelings. / Because...)

Can we write down everything in a day? Then what can we write about?

思维试纸：

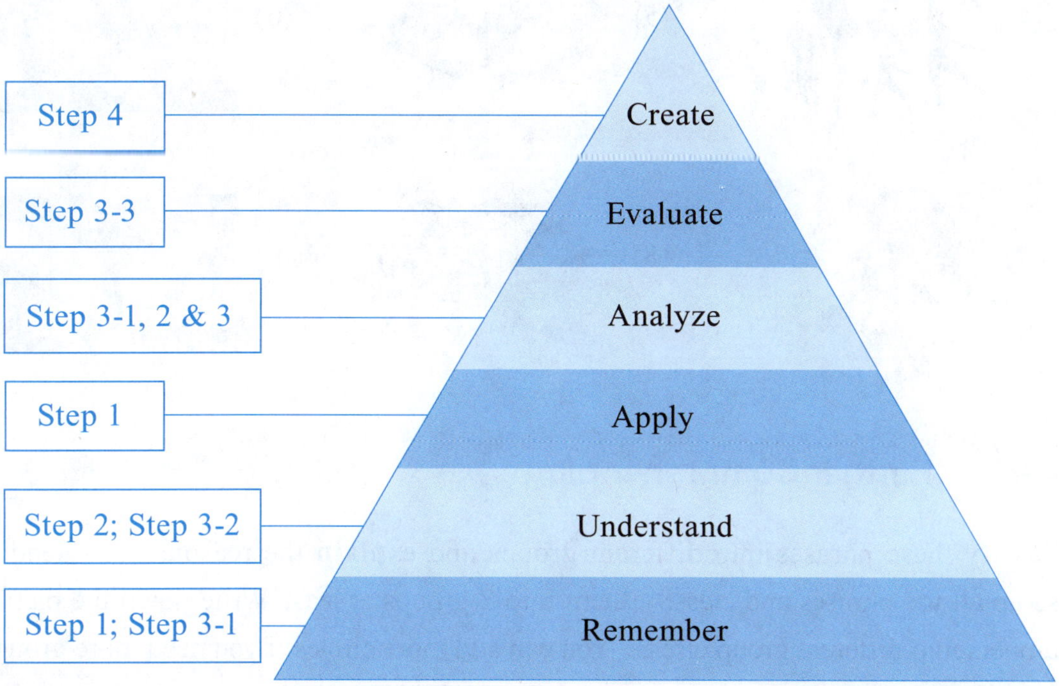

Part Three　Vocabulary

教学素材: Part A & Part B Let's Learn

教学步骤:

Step 1　Checking Your Memory

Match the pictures to the phrases below and each one can be used once only. Write down the matching number of the picture in "(　)".

do morning exercises (　)　eat breakfast (　)　have... class (　)

play sports (　)　eat dinner (　)　clean my room (　)

go for a walk (　)　go shopping (　)　take a dancing class (　)

(1) 

(2) 

(3) 

(4) 

(5) 

(6) 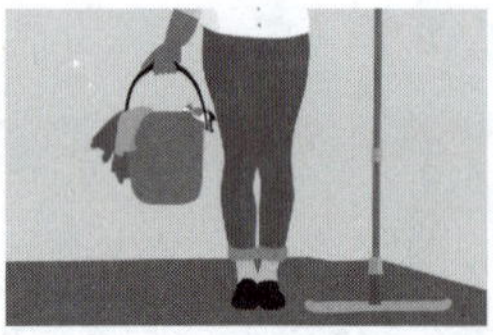

(7) 

(8) 

(9) 

Step 2　Further Comprehending

Classify these phrases into different groups and **explain** the reasons. You need to use up all the phrases and classify them into 2 groups at least. Write down the picture numbers into different group circles. You can add more circles if you need more groups.

Group name: ___________ Group name: ___________

教学时长: 15 mins

教学建议:

词汇部分主要用于练习，旨在巩固词汇和语法知识。学生自行在课前或课后完成。课堂上，学生展示和分享作业，教师纠错。

1. Step 1 为词义匹配活动。教师提醒学生认真读图，短语与图片需一一对应。

参考答案：

(1)；(5)；(2)；(4)；(3)；(6)；(9)；(7)；(8)

2. Step 2不止一个答案。教师可以鼓励学生开动脑筋思考可能的类别，重在解释分类的原因，引导学生探讨分类的好处。如果需要学生练习写这些短语，教师可以把对应数字改成直接写短语。

参考答案：

Indoor activities: (2); (3); (5); (6); (7); (8)

Outdoor activities: (1); (2); (4); (9)

思维试纸:

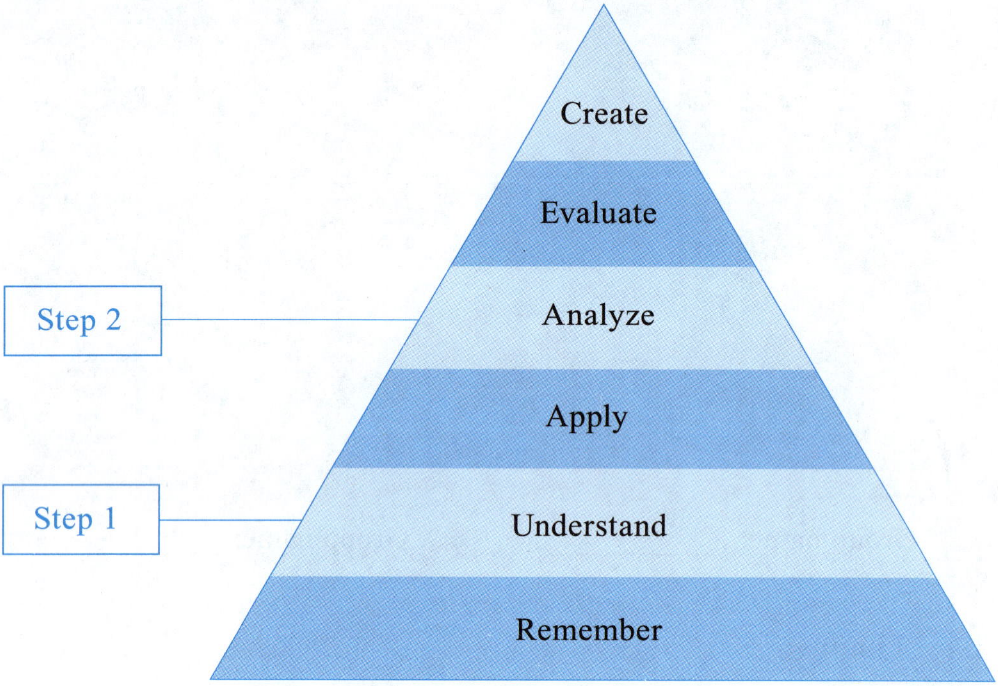

Part Four Grammar

教学素材: sometimes, usually, always, often
教学步骤:

Step 1 Self-checking

1. The words below represent frequency. **Link** them to the matching percentage (%).

sometimes usually always often

100% 80% 60% 40%

2. **Choose** one from "sometimes / often / usually / always" to **fill in** the blanks. And share yours with your partner.
I ________ have dinner at home.

I __________ go shopping.
I __________ have English class.
I __________ clean my room.
（注意：这几个频度词可以重复使用，符合实际情况即可。）

Step 2 Further Practicing

Choose the suitable person / pet to do suitable activities with you. And **make** sentences with the sentence pattern and phrases below.

What do you / they do on the weekend?
__________ (who) __________ (frequency) __________ (activity) with __________ (who) on Saturdays / Sundays.

do morning exercises	**eat breakfast**	**have… class**
play sports	**eat dinner**	**clean my room**
go for a walk	**go shopping**	**take a dancing class**

注意：造句时只替换“sometimes / often / usually / always”几个频度副词，不算新的句子。要根据不同的身份，选择恰当的事情进行匹配，造句意思要合理，要符合常识。

Let's see how many sentences you can make.

Dad Brother Sister Mom Cat Dog

(1) ____________________

(2) ____________________

(3) ____________________

(4) ____________________

(5) ____________________

(6) ____________________

(7) ____________________

教学时长: 15 mins

教学建议:

语法部分主要用于练习，旨在巩固词汇和语法知识。学生自行在课前或课后完成，教师批改。课堂上，教师带领学生总结存在的问题和解决办法。

1. 自我检测环节。

(1) 学生将频率副词和百分数进行连线。

参考答案:

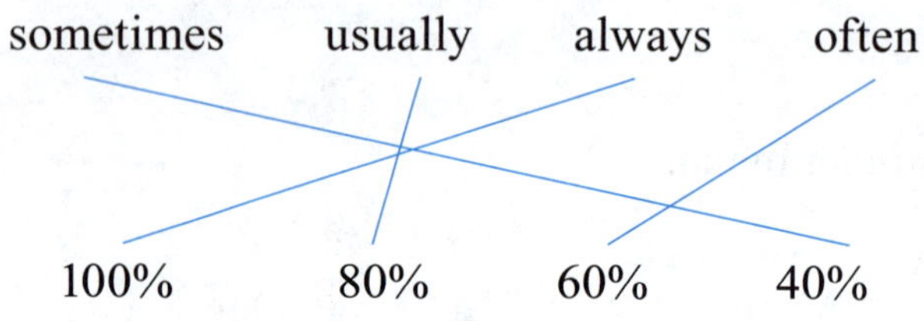

(2) 学生选择频率副词填空。

2. 巩固练习环节。

学生选择合适的人或者宠物一起做活动，并根据所提示的句型进行造句练习。教师需要引导学生根据常识匹配人、物、事件，课堂上可进行造句比赛，提升学生对句子结构的熟悉度。如果学生语言掌握情况较好，教师还可以不限制动作，让学生自行创编句子，甚至创编故事。

思维试纸:

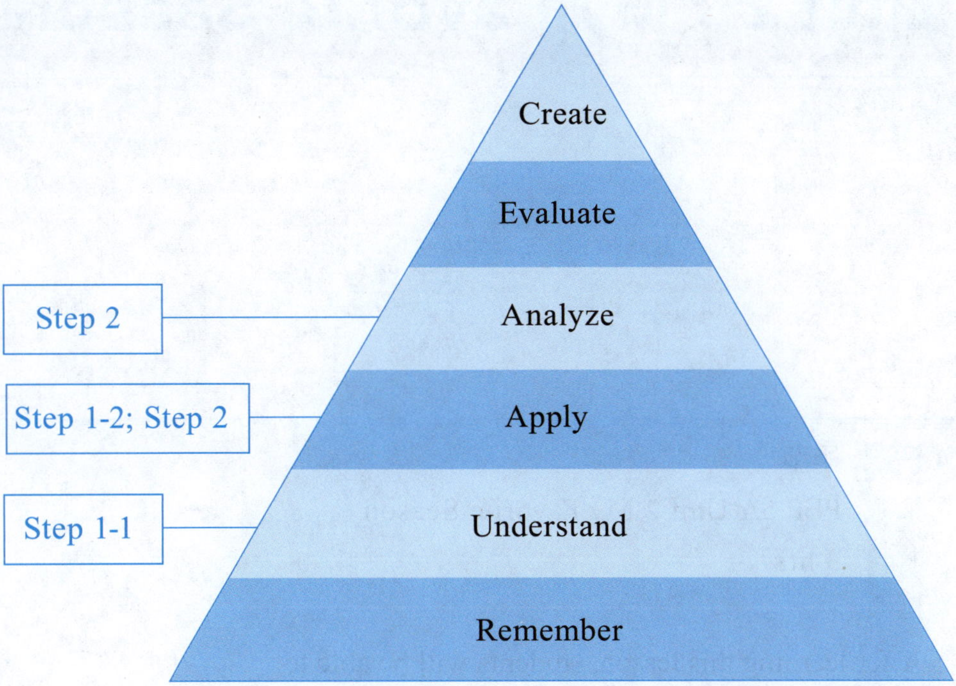
Create
Evaluate
Step 2
Analyze
Step 1-2; Step 2
Apply
Step 1-1
Understand
Remember

Unit 2　My Favorite Season

单元导览

单元话题: 季节
素材来源: PEP 5A Unit 2 My Favorite Season
教学时长: 3 hrs
教学目标:

After learning this lesson, students will be able to

语言目标:

1. **name** four seasons in English (spring, summer, autumn, winter) and **describe** their features by associating expressions about weather, clothes, etc.;

2. **understand** conversations in the textbook and discuss their favorite seasons by **using** vocabulary about seasons and activities in different seasons (make a snowman, pick apples, play in the snow, go on a picnic, plant flowers, eat ice cream, go swimming, etc.);

3. **explain** reasons after **identifying** their favorite seasons by **using** sentence patterns: Which season do you like best? / I like… Because…

4. **comprehend** the meaning of the story, **analyze** the main content and structure by identifying persons and activities on Christmas Day;

5. **write** about the climate, environment and activities of their own hometown on the Spring Festival.

非语言目标:

1. **apply** geographic knowledge about seasons, like how to identify them in both hemispheres;

2. work in groups to finish tasks related to their daily life about seasons and activities;

3. appreciate the beauty of four seasons and their hometowns;

4. **design** logos creatively by associating relevant elements and seasons;

5. **associate** elements about seasons, festivals, activities, environment comprehensively to creatively represent a place.

融思设计

Part One Listening and Speaking

教学素材: Pat B Let's Talk

教学步骤:

Step 1 Listening Comprehension

1. Listen and **fill in** the blank with seasons.

   Miss White likes ____________________ best.

2. **Match** Amy and Miss White to the pictures of their favorite seasons and **recall** the reasons why they like the seasons best. Pictures can give you clues (线索).

Amy

Miss White

Step 2 Preparation before Speaking

1. **Think** which season you like best in Chongqing. Why? Write down your answers in the form below. You can add more aspects by yourself.

	My favorite season in Chongqing is ________.
Weather	It is…
Color	There are…
Activities	I can… with…
Food & Drink	I can eat / drink…
Clothes	I can wear…
Add More	

2. Look at the pictures below. Can you **design** one for your favorite season in Chongqing?

Tip: 下列图片是如何把文字和季节相关的元素结合起来的？先思考，再设计。

Draw your logo here!

Step 3 Speaking and Sharing

1. Each student **ticks** the best season in Chongqing in their own mind.

◇ spring

◇ summer

◇ autumn / fall

◇ winter

2. Discuss in groups and **explain** your decisions in the form below. You can add more aspects by yourself.

Tip: 每个方面要明确写出这个季节不同于其他季节的特点。

We think the best season in Chongqing is ________.

	It is the best, because it is special in… (在……方面是特别的)
Weather	It is…
Color	There are…
Activities	We can… with…
Food & Drink	We can eat / drink…
Clothes	We can wear…

3. Choose one of your pictures to **revise** and make it better. **Draw** it here.

教学时长: 1.5 hrs

教学建议:

1. 听力理解环节。

教师播放录音，学生完成练习。教师根据学生完成情况可再播放一遍，并进行校对。

Miss White likes summer best.

2. 表达准备环节：教师安排学生在课前完成。

3. 表达与分享环节。

（1）教师布置学生课前完成题单，课堂上检查学生完成情况 。

（2）教师将学生分成四人小组后说明任务：需要讨论出小组公认的重庆最好的季节并说明理由。

各小组成员先根据自己的想法在题单上面勾选出心目中最好的季节，然后进行讨论，并填写表格，重点填写这个季节特殊的方面。教师可根据学生水平决定是否举例说明。如果小组成员能想到更多的方面，可自行补充。

（3）分析完成后，各小组挑选出最佳设计图并进行修改完善；如果没有，可安排重新设计。

小组自愿向全班展示。展示时，教师注意引导学生使用目标语言，例如：

We think the best season in Chongqing is spring. It is the best because there are many flowers. They are yellow, pink, blue, orange…

其他学生表态：I agree. / I disagree.

教师邀请学生简要说明理由。

教师带领学生总结：最喜欢的不一定是最好的。首先要勇于表态，然后做出自己的判断；判断时需要基于具体的原因。判断哪些方面最好的时候，应考虑区别于其他同类事物的特殊优点。

思维试纸:

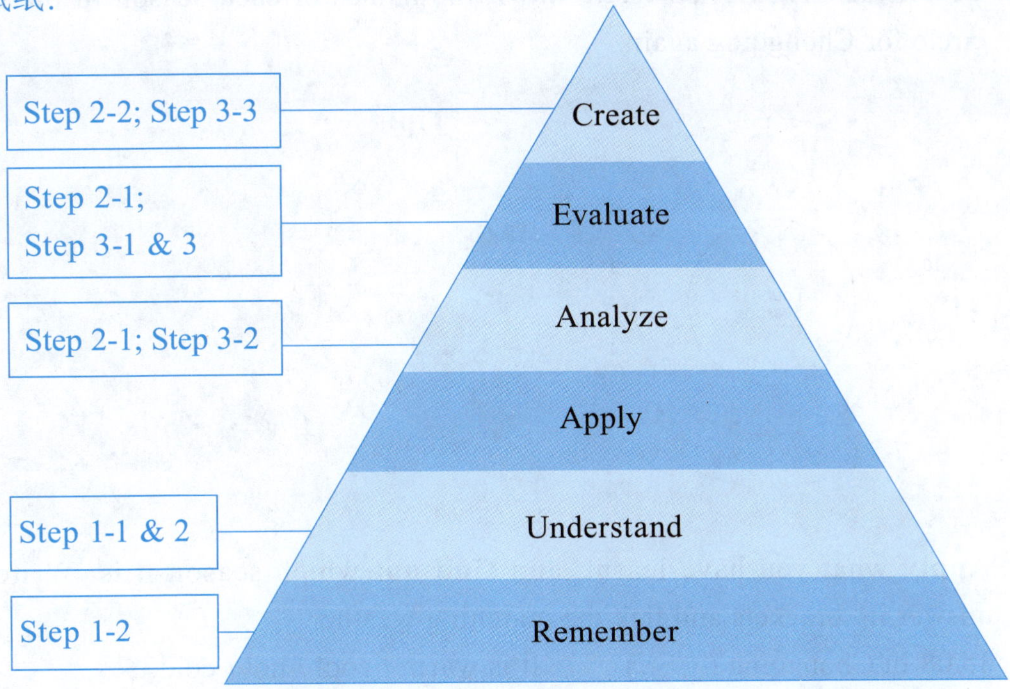

Part Two Reading and Writing

教学素材: Part B Story Time

教学步骤:

Step 1 Preparation before Reading

1. When are "four seasons" in Chongqing? Based on your knowledge, **recall** the name of each season in the middle circle for Chongqing.

   For example:

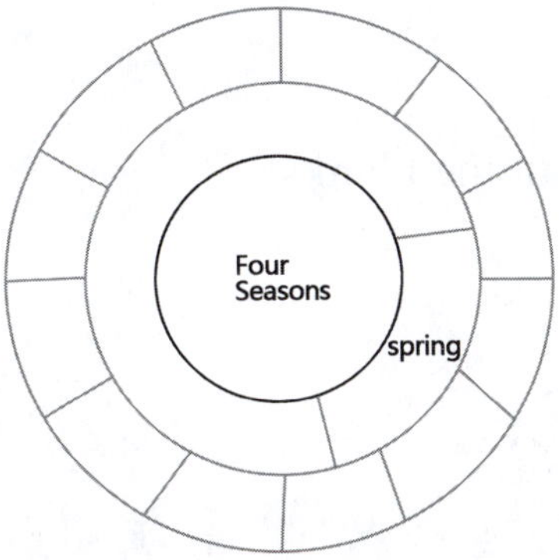

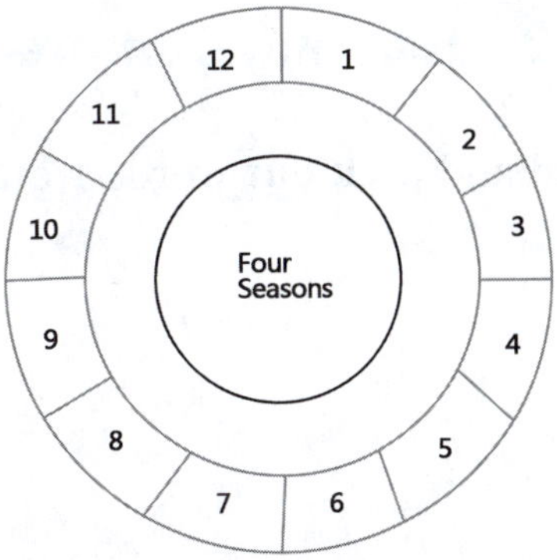

2. **Learn** the "Tip". Then **write down** the names of each season in the middle circle for Chongqing again.

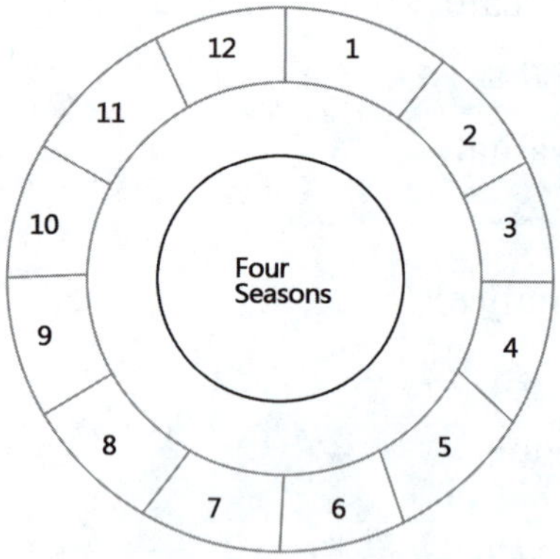

Tip:

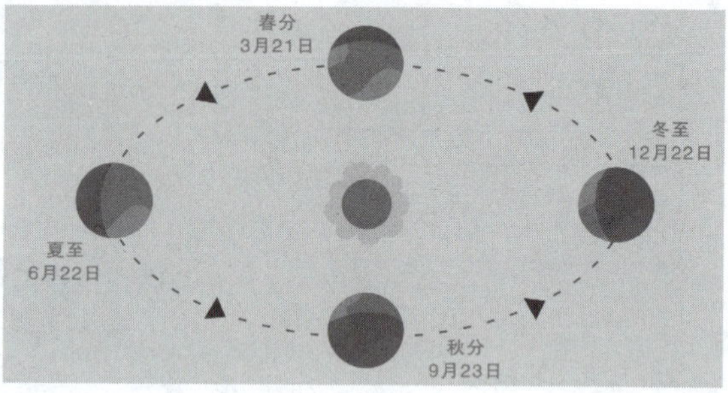

3. **Apply** what you have learnt, and **find out** which season it is. Write your answer in brackets and tick the matching weather.

15/08 in Chongqing ( ) It is warm / cool / hot / cold.

01/10 in Beijing ( ) It is warm / cool / hot / cold.

24/01 in Canada ( ) It is warm / cool / hot / cold.

4. **Test** your partner.

__________ in __________ is __________.

It is __________.

5. **Challenge** yourself!

02/02 in Thailand ( )

It is warm / cool / hot / cold.

12/25 in Australia ( )

It is warm / cool / hot / cold.

Step 2 Reading Comprehension

1. Read and **pick out** words from the box to fill in the blanks.

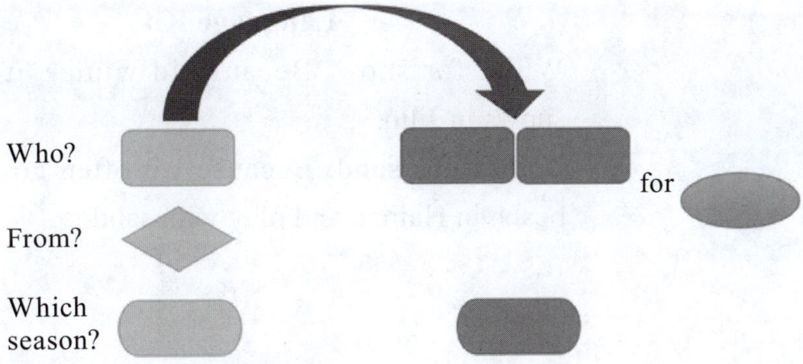

Koala Zip Zoom
Christmas Day
Australia: winter / summer

2. **Read** again and **answer** the questions.

(1) Which season does Koala like?

A. Spring. B. Summer. C. Autumn. D. Winter.

(2) What doesn't Koala do on Christmas Day?

A. Go to the beach. B. Swim in the sea. C. Make a snowman.

Why? ______________________________

Step 3 Preparation before Writing

Recall and **compare** the colors you see on the Spring Festival in Jilin province and Hainan province in China and fill in the form below.

Hainan

Jilin

Language Kit

White for snow. Because in winter, it often snows in Jilin.

Yellow for sand. Because we often go to the beach in Hainan and play with sand.

…

Jilin	Hainan

ALIKE

Red for lanterns (灯笼)

____

____

DIFFERENT

White for snow	Yellow for sand
______________	______________
______________	______________
______________	______________
______________	______________

Step 4 Writing and Sharing

Choose colors to best **represent** the Spring Festival for your hometown. **Write** about them and **explain** the reasons of your choices.

____

I think ____________________ (colors) can represent the Spring Festival for my hometown ________________ (province or city name). _______________ is for ______________; _____ is for _____________; _________________ is for ____________

____

____

I choose them because ________________________________

____

____

____

(climate / activities / environment).

Language Kit

Climate: It is… / It… / It has… in winter.

Activities: We make a snowman / have dinner with family… on the Spring Festival.

Environment: There are… flowers / trees…

教学时长：1 hr

教学建议：

1. 读前准备环节。

(1) 学生回想四季的单词，激活思维。

(2) 教师补充新知，关联地理学科知识，引导学生判断四季的划分。

(3) 学生在新的语境应用新知，判断国内外不同地区的季节，关联与季节相应的天气的表达。

参考答案：

summer, hot; autumn, cool; winter, cold

（4）学生通过给同伴出题，加深对新知的理解，同时增加目标单词的使用频率，教师鼓励学生练习自己使用有困难的季节单词。

（5）教师鼓励学生进一步挑战自己，对泰国和澳大利亚的季节进行判断；然后邀请学生分享答案，解释原因；最后建议学生去探索其他判断季节的方法，但是一定要有依据。

参考答案：

summer, hot; summer, hot

2. 阅读理解环节。

（1）教师引导全班阅读理解文本：Do you know what festival is it on December 25th? Yes, Christmas. Today, we're going to read a story about Christmas. The story is about Koala, Zip and Zoom's new friend. Do you know where does Koala come from? Yes, Australia!

教师提示学生首先分析图形的含义，箭头代表着方向和目的，不同形状的图块代表着不同类别的信息。学生将方框中的单词分类。然后，教师再引导学生根据对文本信息的理解，完成图示。

教师引导学生根据图示，总结这个故事的主要内容。

参考答案：

Koala, Zip, Zoom; Australia, Christmas Day; summer, winter

（2）学生自行阅读并回答问题，检查对细节的理解，教师可以邀请学生回答和分享。

参考答案：

（1）B　（2）C

Because Christmas is in summer in Australia.

3. 写作准备环节。

教师引导学生思考吉林和海南这两个地方在春节时是什么气候，有什么特殊的庆祝方式，又有什么共同之处。学生分组填表，看哪个组写得多。同一个颜色可以代表不同的事物。

4. 写作与分享环节。

教师鼓励学生思考在春节时哪些颜色最能够代表自己的家乡，体现家乡的气候、风景或者节日风俗。学生独立写作。写作任务可以在课后完成，下节课再分享。

思维试纸:

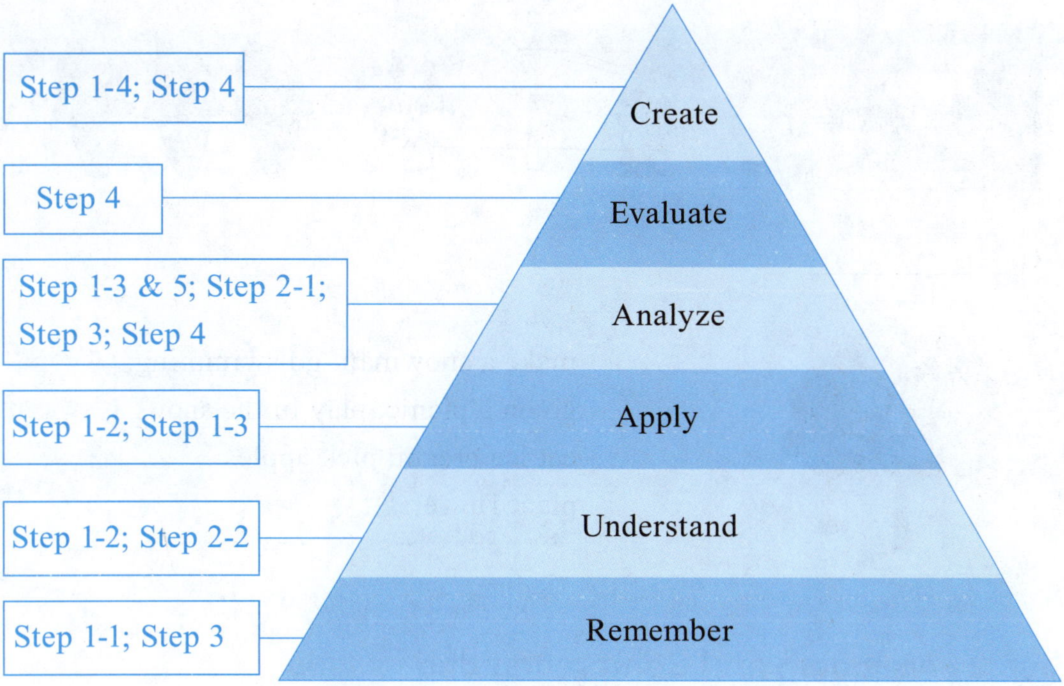

Part Three Vocabulary

教学素材: Part A & Part B Let's Learn

教学步骤:

Step 1 Checking Your Memory

Select phrases from the box and **match** them to these pictures.

A. ______________ B. ______________ C. ______________

D. ______________ E. ______________ F. ______________

G. ______________

make a snowman; go swimming;
go on a picnic; play in the snow;
eat ice cream; pick apples
plant flowers

Step 2 Matching and Comprehending

Analyze clues and write down the seasons or activities in the first two rows.

Seasons	Activities	Places
	plant flowers, go on a picnic	Chongqing
	pick apples	Beijing
summer		Yunnan
winter		Sydney

Step 3 Using Vocabulary

1. Answer the question "Which season do you like best?" **Recall** and fill in the blank.

I like ____________ best.

2. **Select** the phrases in Step 1 to **explain** your idea, and write down the letters (字母) in the blank.

Because I can ____.

3. **Write down** other reasons.

Because ____

____.

教学时长: 15 mins

教学建议:

词汇部分主要用于练习，旨在巩固词汇和语法知识。学生自行在课前或课后完成，教师批改。课堂上，教师带领学生总结存在原问题和解决办法。

Step 1 主要是图文匹配；Step 2 要将地点和季节性活动结合起来推断季节；Step 3 旨在引导学生将季节、活动的单词、短语关联到一起。

参考答案：

Step 1: go swimming, make a snowman, plant flowers, go on a picnic, play in the snow, eat ice-cream, pick apples

Step 2: spring; autumn; go swimming, eat ice cream, go on a picnic; go swimming, eat ice cream, go on a picnic（答案不唯一，言之成理即可。）

Step 3: 言之成理即可。

思维试纸:

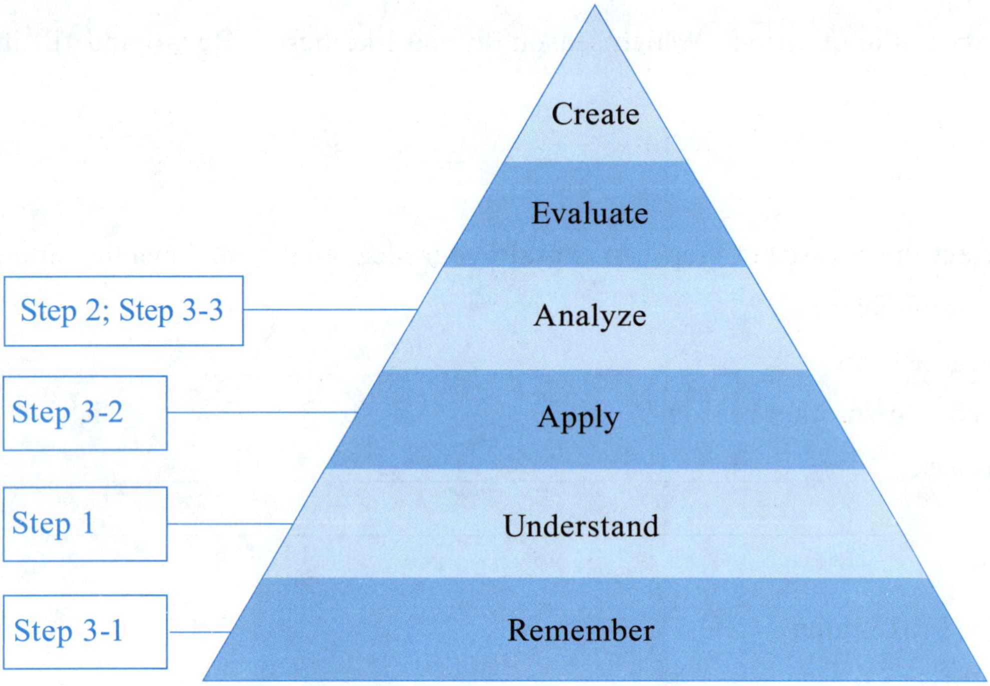

Part Four　Grammar

教学素材: Part A & Part B Let's Learn

教学步骤:

Step 1　Self-checking

Analyze the pictures below and **make** sentences with "what", "when", "where", "which" and "why".

(1)

— ____?

— ______________________________ is in the box.

(2) 

— ______________________________?

— I like ______________________________ best.

— ______________________________?

— Because ______________________________.

(3) 

— ______________________________?

— I wake up ______________________________.

(4) 

— ______________________________ on the weekend?

— I often ______________________________.

Step 2 Rule-finding

Circle what shares in the sentences and fill in the blanks. Cross the words of the first column.

疑问的部分 | ______ | 动作

Who Which… Where Why What

疑问的部分 | ______ | 人/物 | 地点

Who Which… Where Why What

Step 3 Further Practicing

Students can work in pairs and **use** question and answer to **draw** a picture including: who, when, where, what.

教学时长: 15 mins

教学建议:

语法部分主要用于练习，学生自行在课前或课后完成，教师批改。课堂上，教师带领学生总结存在的问题和解决办法。

1. Step 1: 教师引导学生分析图片及句子线索，根据图片内容，运用what/when/where/which/why提问，完成填空。

参考答案:

(1) — Who is in the box?

— The boy is in the box.

(2) — Which season do you like best?

— I like winter best.

(3) — Why do you like winter best?

— Because we can play in the snow. (其他理由也可。)

(4) — When do you wake up?

— I wake up at about 7 o'clock.

(5) — What do you often do on the weekend?

— I often go swimming. (其他符合图片的答案也可。)

2. Step 2: 教师引导学生分析句子，找出运用what / who / where / which / why提问的句子结构，总结存在的问题和解决办法。

3. Step 3: 学生通过问答画出彼此心中的图画，问答内容包含时间、地点、人物、事件，学生也可以自行拓展。教师可以先邀请一位同学做示范，再让学生自行练习。

思维试纸：

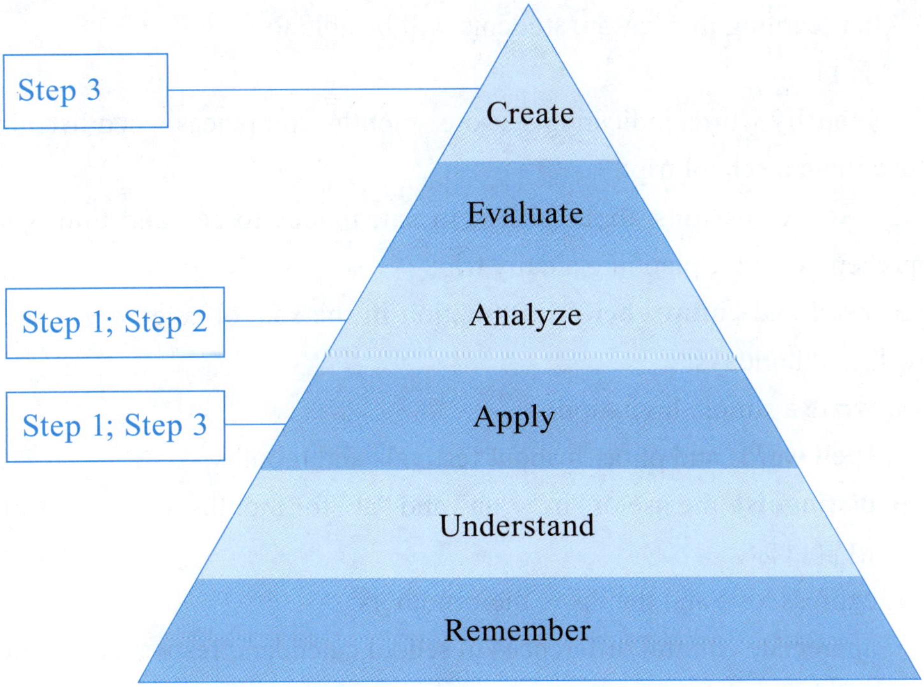

Unit 3 My School Calendar

单元导览

单元话题: 校历
素材来源: PEP 5A Unit 3 My School Calendar
教学时长: 3 hrs
教学目标:

After learning this lesson, students will be able to

语言目标:

1. **identify** words indicating seasons, months and places when listening to the text about a school trip;

2. **use** expressions about places to eat, places to see and things to do comprehensively for planning a daily trip;

3. **read** and **comprehend** information in the school calendar, especially festivals and holidays;

4. **write** a simple invitation;

5. **spell** words and phrases about festivals and months;

6. **distinguish** the use of "in", "on" and "at" for months, dates and time.

非语言目标:

1. express love and thanks to their mothers;

2. appreciate cultural differences in school calendars, festivals and holidays between China and America;

3. reasonably **make** trip plans based on the purpose of the trip;

4. **compare** similarities and differences to make a better decision;

5. **evaluate** choices of months to select the most suitable one.

融思设计

Part One Listening and Speaking

教学素材: Part A Let's Talk

教学步骤:

Step 1 Preparation before Listening

There is a school trip in Beijing. Can you **guess** when and where students will go? Write down your ideas in the columns below. You can draw if you do not know the words.

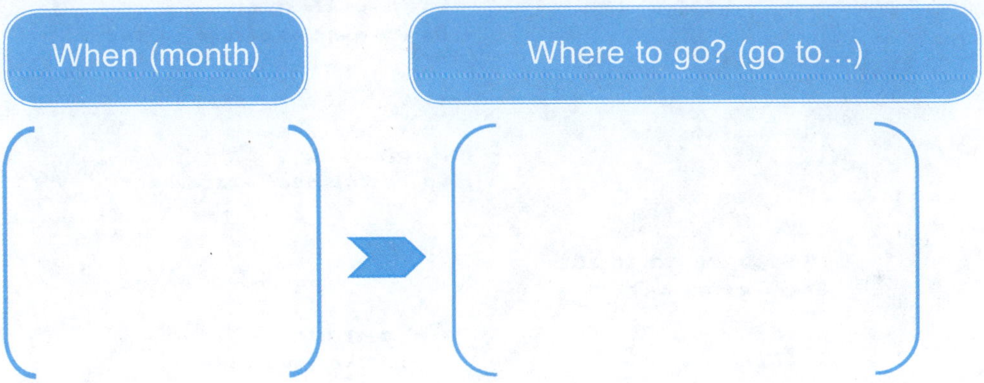

Step 2 Listening Comprehension

Listen and **fill in** the columns.

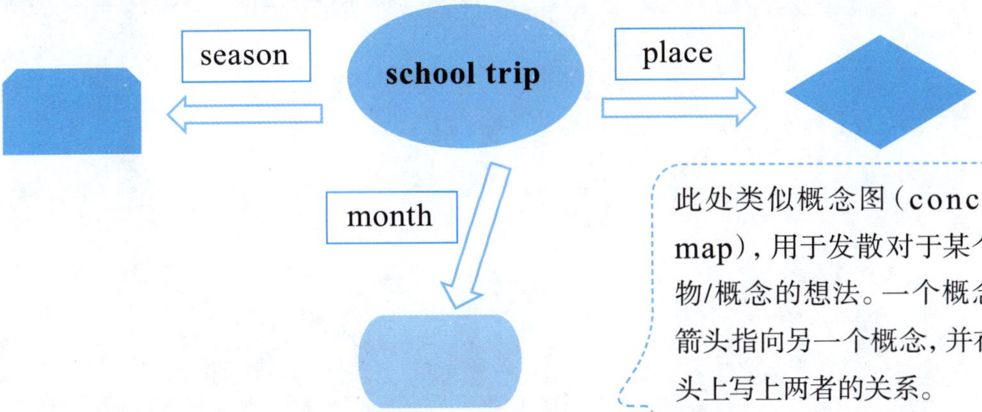

此处类似概念图(concept map),用于发散对于某个事物/概念的想法。一个概念用箭头指向另一个概念,并在箭头上写上两者的关系。

Step 3　Preparation before Speaking

Identify and circle what are included for planning a day trip.

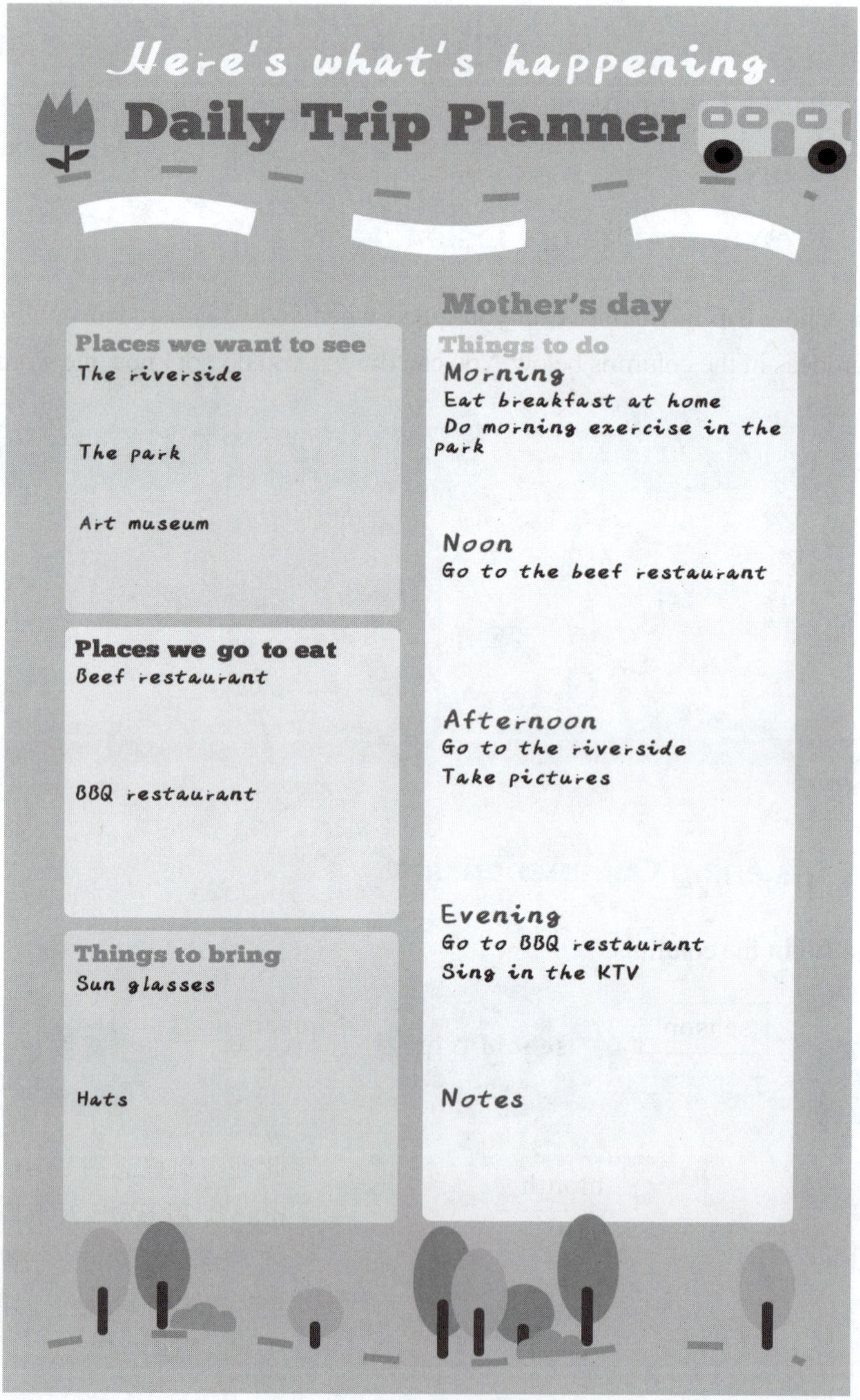

Step 4 Speaking and Sharing

1. **Brainstorm** and **analyze** what your mom likes and what she dislikes.

Likes	Dislikes

2. **Design** a trip plan for your mom to celebrate Mother's Day.

海报中要包含“Daily Trip Planner”的主要内容。

教学时长: 1.5 hrs

教学建议:

1. 听前准备环节。

教师展示北京的图片，介绍教材中的主人公学校要组织一次郊游。教师提问: Have you been to Beijing? When? Where have you been to? 逐步过渡到: Can you guess when and where students will go?

这个过程中，学生可能会缺少关于北京名胜古迹的词汇，教师可以让学生用自己已知的语言给出线索，教师来补充英文和中文。

2. 听力理解环节。

播放录音前，教师提醒学生读图，注意听关键词（season, month, place），以及提问时会出现的重点词（which season, which month, where）。教师播放录音，学生填写。教师核对答案: autumn; October; the Great Wall。

3. 表达准备环节。

学生自行读图，然后和同伴讨论要计划一天的郊游，需要包含哪些内容；教师提问: After your observation, what should be included for a day trip?

学生可以一起回答。

教师总结: When we plan a trip, we need to decide the time, things to do, places to see, places to eat and things to bring. Can you think of other things we need to consider?

该环节教师应引导学生尽可能从多个方面进行思考。

4. 表达与分享环节。

（1）教师引导学生回忆自己妈妈喜欢和不喜欢的事物，填写表格；教师提问: When you celebrate Mother's Day, should you do things your mom likes or dislikes? 教师引导学生尽量选择妈妈喜欢的活动，避开她不喜欢的事物，然后过渡到为妈妈计划一天的郊游。

（2）学生两人或四人一组，讨论应该如何设计郊游计划，怎么安排各项活动，彼此交流想法；商量完成后，各自完成自己的郊游计划。

学生在组内用英语介绍自己设计的郊游计划；教师邀请小组在全班分享。

思维试纸:

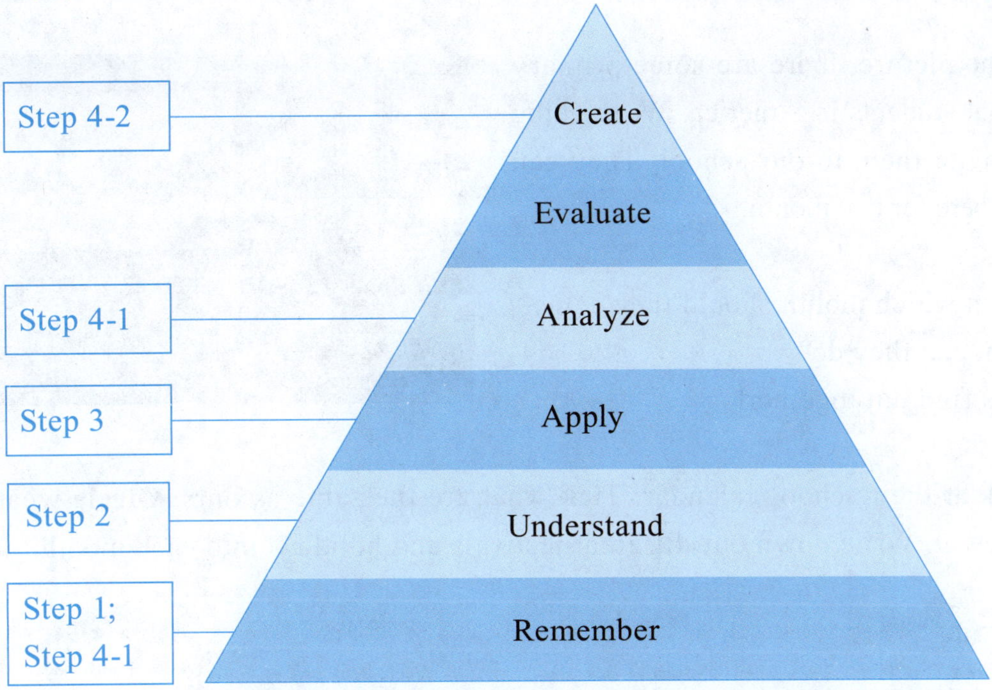

Part Two Reading and Writing

教学素材: Part B Read and Write

教学步骤:

Step 1 Preparation before Reading

Recall festivals and holidays and write them down on your school calendar.

School Calendar

January	February	March	April	May	June
July	**August**	**September**	**October**	**November**	**December**

Step 2 Reading Comprehension

In the picture, there are some primary school students in America. We're going to invite them to our school. They can stay here for one month.

But in which month should they come?
What can they do?
Let's find out together!

Look at their school calendar. **Tick** what are the same as ours. **Circle** what are different. Write down our different festivals and holidays into each month.

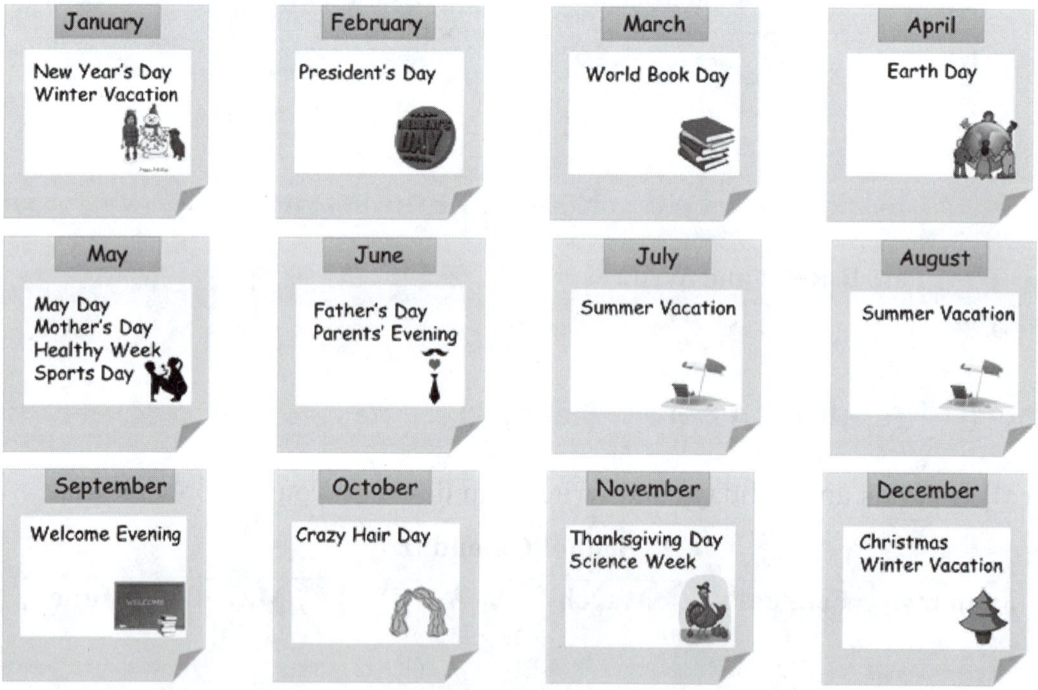

Step 3 Preparation before Writing

Select the best three months for those American primary school students to come. **Explain** the reasons.

1 Because we will… We have… It is…

2 Because…

3 Because…

Step 4 Writing and Sharing

Choose the best month and **write** the invitation.

You are invited!

When:
Why:

Where:
What:

教学时长: 1 hr

教学建议:

1. 读前准备环节。

学生回忆一年都有哪些节假日，可以独自完成，也可以小组讨论完成。

2. 阅读理解环节。

教师说明任务：有一群美国小学生要来学校交流参观，需要学生决定他们什么时候来，来了之后要做些什么。为了更好地做决定，首先，教师展示美国小学的校历，引导学生识别节假日，对学生不熟悉的重要的节日做一定的讲解，如总统日、读书日。然后，教师提示学生将其和自己的校历进行比较，勾出一样的，圈出不一样的。教师邀请学生分享，哪些不一样，为什么不一样。

3. 写作准备环节。

学生分组讨论，将最适合美国小学生来交流的三个月份选出来，并说明原因。教师可以做示范：

June is good because we have Children's Day. We will dance and sing songs. We will have many gifts. It is fun.

4. 写作与分享环节。

首先，教师带学生再次熟悉教材上的邀请函的文本，了解when / why / where / what后面都分别要写些什么。学生小组分享，选出组内最有吸引力的邀请函。然后，全班分享，每个小组分享完之后教师问其他小组是否喜欢，喜欢的话就竖起大拇指。教师可以在黑板上画爱心等，最后选出全班最受欢迎的邀请函。

思维试纸：

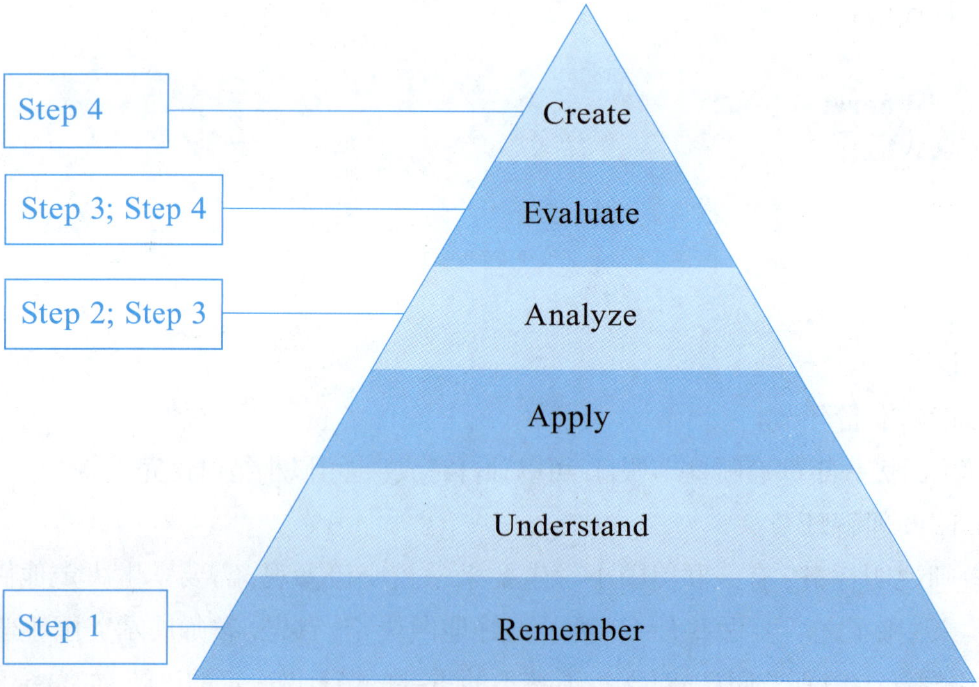

Part Three Vocabulary

教学素材: Part A & Part B Let's Learn

教学步骤:

Step 1 Word-checking

Put months into the right column and **correct** the wrong spellings.

March →	June →	______ →	Decembe
↑			↑
______			______
↑			↑
Janury →	______ →	Jully →	October

Step 2 Naming and Matching

Write down the festival name under each picture. **Match** festivals to months. Write down the numbers of months beside the festivals.

(1) __________

(2) __________

(3) __________

(4) __________

(5) __________

(6) __________

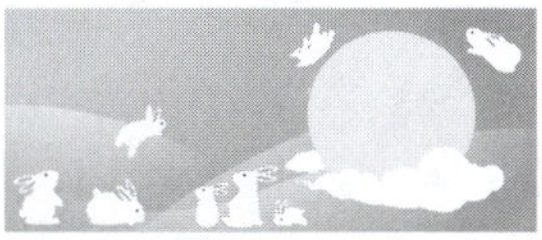

(7) __________

(8) __________

Step 3 Further Associating

Choose one month and list the festivals below. Let's compete who can **think of** the most festivals and **recall** relevant (相关的) activities.

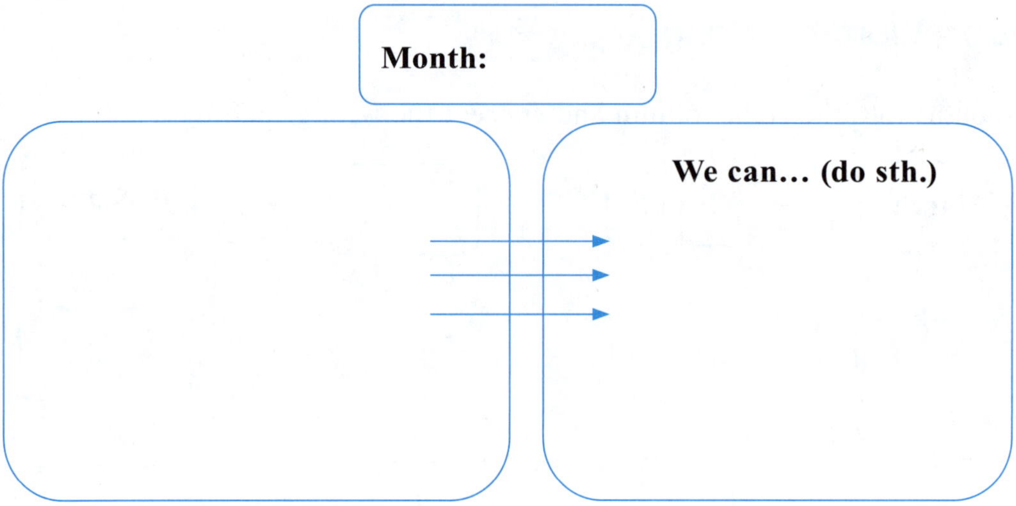

教学时长：15 mins

教学建议：

词汇部分主要用于练习，旨在巩固词汇和语法知识。学生自行在课前或课后完成。课堂上，学生展示和分享作业，教师纠错。

1. Step 1：学生根据已有的线索推测出方框中的月份，并校对拼写。课堂上，教师可以借助PPT 或者板书进行反馈。

参考答案（答案不唯一）：

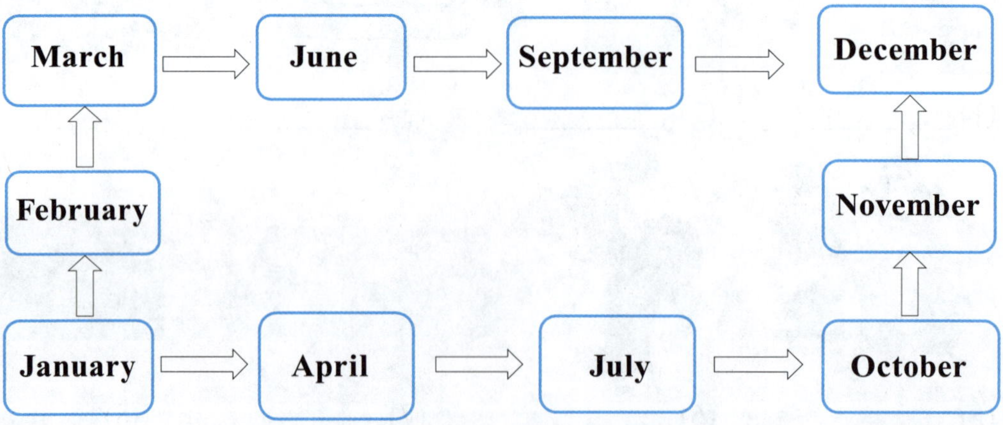

2. Step 2：学生看图写节日，并写出该节日所在月份的数字。如果课堂上练习的话，教师可以直接询问学生：Which month is…?

参考答案：

(1) Teachers' Day (9)
(2) Father's Day (6)
(3) the Dragon Boat Festival (6)
(4) Christmas Day (12)
(5) the Spring Festival (1/2)
(6) Mother's Day (5)
(7) Mid-autumn Day (9)
(8) China's National Day (10)

3. Step 3：学生思考并找出节日最多的月份，关联可以做的事情。

思维试纸：

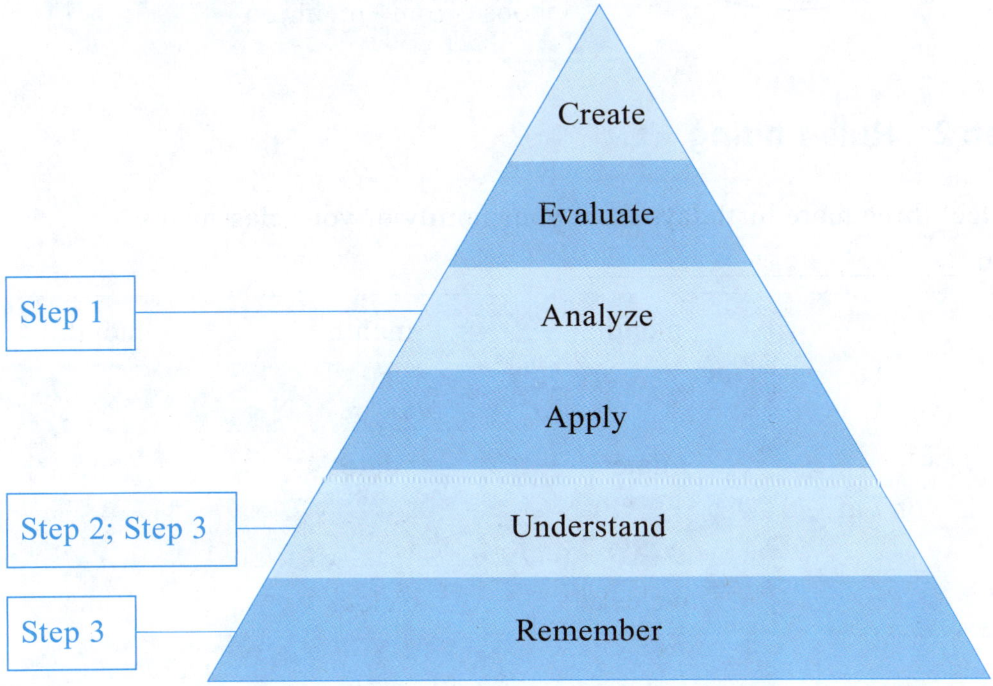

Part Four　Grammar

教学素材: Part B Let's Learn

教学步骤:

Step 1　Self-checking

Recall your birthday and fill in the blanks.

When is your birthday?

It is ________ ________;

It is ___on___ ________;

It is ________ ________ o'clock.

Choose from "in, at, on".

Step 2　Rule-finding

Collect three more birthdays from your family or your classmates.

Who: ____________________

in / on / at	month	month	month
	date	date	date
	o'clock	o'clock	o'clock

Step 3　Further Practicing

You are going to hold a birthday party for these three persons together. **Choose** the time and answer the questions by filling in the blanks.

When is the birthday party?

_________ (month) _________ (date) __________ (o'clock).

Because ____.

What will you do?

We will ____.

教学时长: 15 mins

教学建议:

学生自行在课前或课后完成，教师批改。课堂上，教师带领学生总结存在的问题和解决办法。

1. Step 1: 学生回忆自己的出生日期，并将答案填写在横线上。

2. Step 2: 学生搜集并填写三个人的出生日期，可以是家人也可以是同学的出生日期。

3. Step 3: 学生要举行一个生日派对，需要填写正确的日期和时间，并写出理由，最后填写派对上的活动。

三个练习都没有唯一的答案，教师主要引导学生总结出月份与in、日期与on、时间与 at 搭配，以及will表示将要发生的事情。

思维试纸:

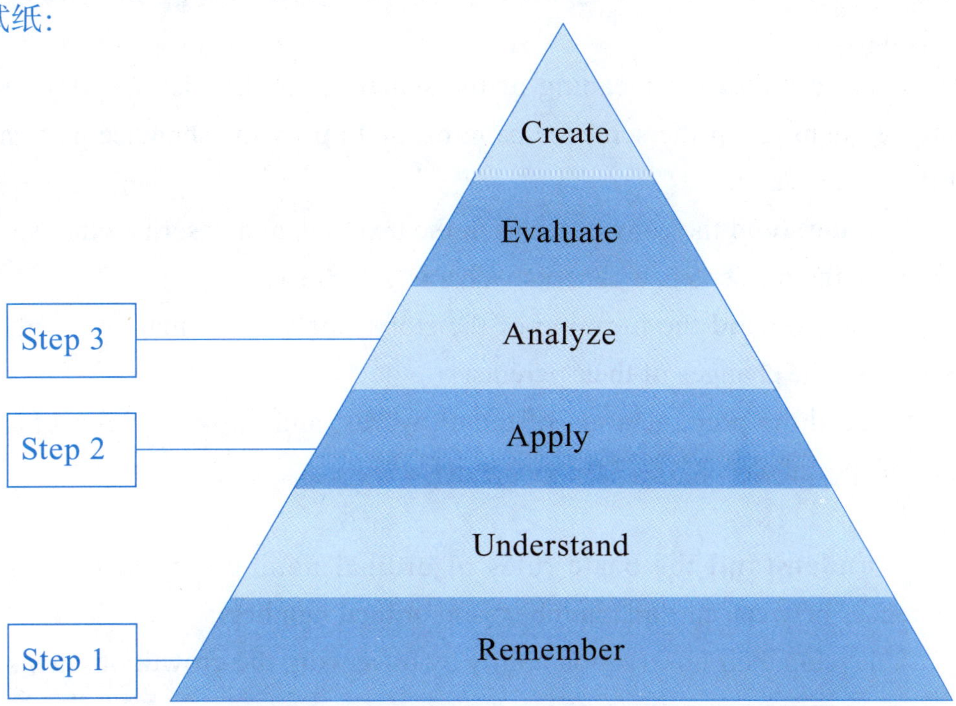

Unit 4 When Is the Art Show?

单元导览

单元话题：旅行活动
素材来源：PEP 5B Unit 4 When Is the Art Show?
教学时长：3 hrs
教学目标：

By the end of the lessons, students will be able to

语言目标：

1. **understand** the meaning of the words (first, second, third, fourth, fifth, twelfth, twentieth, twenty-first, twenty-second) and **apply** to writing and speaking;

2. **understand** the meaning of the sentences (When is…? / It's on…), **analyze** the usage of the sentence patterns, and **apply** the sentence patterns to writing and speaking;

3. **understand** the conversations in the textbook and describe other special days by **using** the sentence patterns: What is…? / It's on…

4. **comprehend** the meaning of the story, **analyze** the main content, and write about the changes of their parents;

5. recall the pronunciation of month words, and **apply** to describing the dates of special days.

非语言目标：

1. **understand** the basic rules of ordinal numbers by analyzing the differences between cardinal numbers and ordinal numbers;

2. develop their observation ability by **observing** the growth of kittens and

the changes of their parents to stimulate their caring to others;

3. cultivate their divergent thinking by giving open questions and **designing** a poster;

4. work in groups to finish tasks and to learn from others;

5. strengthen their higher order thinking skills: **analyzing**, **evaluating** and **creating** by planning an event to attract other students.

融思设计

Part One Listening and Speaking

教学素材: Part A Let's Talk

教学步骤:

Step 1 Preparation before Listening

Look and **identify** the date.

May 2020						
Sun	Mon	Tue	Wed	Thu	Fri	Sat
					1	2
3	4	5	6	7	8	9
10	11	12	13	14	15	16
17	18	19	20	21	22	23
24	25	26	27	28	29	30
31						

When is May Day?

May Day is on ____________ ____________.

Step 2 Listening Comprehension

1. **Recall** and write down the special days in May.

____.

2. Listen and **judge** the statements are True or False.

( ) (1) The art show is on May 3rd.

( ) (2) May Day is on May 1st.

( ) (3) The reading festival is on May 7th.

3. Do you know other special days? **Recall**, fill in the blanks and share.

I know ____.

Time: It is on ____.

Place: We often ______________________________________.

Activity: We can _____________________________________.

Step 3 Preparation before Speaking

1. We have some special events in June. You are invited to choose one and plan an event for our class.

Events in June			
Children's Day 	Environment Day 	the Dragon Boat Festival 	Father's Day 

2. **Plan** your festival and **fill in** the blanks. Try to attract the guests.

(1) What event do you choose to plan?

We choose ____________________.

(2) When is it?

It's on ______________________,

because ______________________

______________________________.

(3) Where will it be held?

It's ______________________.

(4) What activities do you have?

We have ______________________

______________________.

singing show, kung fu show, dance competition, you do and I guess...

(5) What can the guests do?

They can ______________________

____

______________________.

dance, sing, draw, write, do kung fu, eat, drink, watch TV, listen to music, run, jump, cook, play football / basketball...

3. Let's **make** a poster for your event. **Draw** and **write**. You should cover information from the 5 questions in Exercise 2.

Invitation

Event:

Date:

Place:

Activities:

You can:

Step 4 Speaking and Sharing

1. Let's **share** and invite your classmates to join in your event. The more stars you get, the more popular your party is! Let's see: whose event is the most attractive.

Speaking pattern:

Dear friends,

Welcome to our ________. It's on ________. It's ________.
We have ________ for you. You can ______________________.

Please join us!

Invitation

2. Count the stars and **choose** the most attractive group.

Children's Day	Environment Day	the Dragon Boat Festival	Father's Day

Group ________	Group ________	Group ________	Group ________

教学时长: 1.5 hrs

教学建议:

1. 听前准备环节。

学生通过观察日历, 复习日期的表达, 填写日期。在学生完成句子填写之后, 教师可以呈现更多的节日, 询问学生: When is…?

2. 听力理解环节。

(1) 学生听录音, 写出短文中的两个节日单词。

参考答案:

the art show; the reading festival

(2) 学生听录音, 完成判断题。

参考答案:

(1) F (2) T (3) F

(3) 教师引导学生填写他们所知道的其他节日, 在什么时候, 一般在哪里, 会做些什么。学生进行小组分享。

3. 表达准备环节。

(1) 活动策划: 教师呈现六月 (也可更换成其他月份, 根据实际情况而定) 的日历, 呈现学校将在该月举行的活动, 让学生进行计划和设计。该活动为小组活动, 教师分配活动给不同的小组, 组员需要讨论回答所列的五个问题, 并且思考哪些活动具有吸引力。

(2) 教师说明学生需要在规定的时间内，以小组为单位完成一张海报，海报内容要包括所列的五个方面。

4. 表达与分享环节。

(1) 小组完成海报后，小组成员需要进行分享。

分享建议一：学生小组重新分组，保证每个小组内的成员都来自不同的小组，然后组内依次进行分享，新小组成员投票并画星星，说明投票的理由。分享结束后，学生回到最初的小组进行总结。

分享建议二：小组依次上台进行分享，其他小组投票并画星星，教师可邀请部分学生说明投票的理由，小组成员不给自己小组投票。

(2) 小组得到的星星越多，代表小组活动策划越吸引人，选出最佳策划组。

思维试纸：

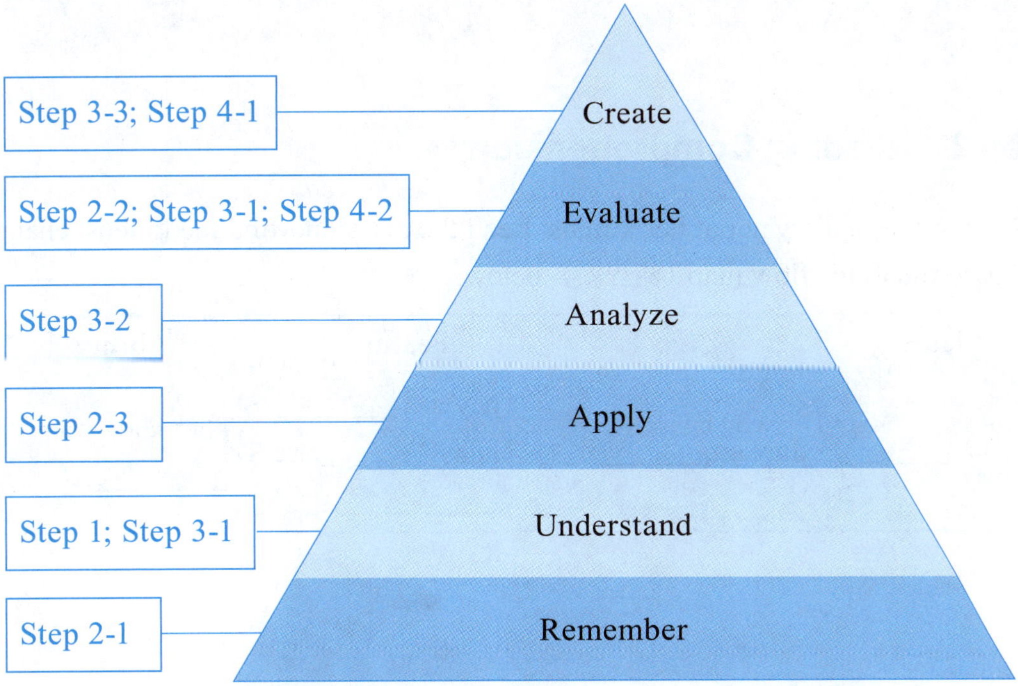

Part Two Reading and Writing

教学素材: Part B Read and Write
教学步骤:

Step 1 Preparation before Reading

Sarah has some new kittens. Here are some pictures of the kittens. **Order** these pictures and draw a line.

April 21st　　April 15th　　April 26th　　May 3rd

Step 2 Reading Comprehension

1. Sarah writes a diary about her kittens. Read the diary and find the kittens' changes. Please **finish** the flow map（流程图）below.

Time	Age	Feature	Ability
On ________	they are ________	They are ________. Their ________ are ________.	They can / can't ________.

2. **Investigate** the answers according to Sarah's diary in the textbook.

(1) Sarah has ________ new kitten(s).

A. one B. two C. three

(2) Kittens are ________ because they are very young.

A. pink B. blue C. white

(3) On April 21st, they can ________.

A. run B. make noise C. walk

(4) Their eyes are open on ________.

A. April 15th B. May 3rd C. April 26th

(5) The kittens can walk on ________.

A. April 15th B. May 26th C. May 3rd

Step 3 Writing and Sharing

1. **Choose** 2 pictures showing your mom's or dad's changes and **sequence** (排序) the pictures according to the age, and then fill in these blanks.

a photo of him/her before you were born

a photo for now

____________ (age)

____________ (age)

____ is _________.
______ is / are _______. (feature)

____ is _________.
______ is / are _______. (feature)

2. What are his / her changes? Please observe and **summarize**.

Changes	Before	Now
appearance: (He / She is…) (His / Her… is / are…)		
abilities: (He / She can… / can't…)		

3. **Write** a diary for your mom / dad now.

You should consider:

When is it today?

How old is he / she?

What is he / she like?

What can he / she do?

What can't he / she do?

What does he / she like?

What do you want to say to him / her?

4. **Share** your diary with your group members voluntarily.

教学时长: 1 hr

教学建议:

1. 读前准备环节。

教师引导学生通过观察小猫的外貌或者行为，将小猫图片与时间匹配，激发学生的学习兴趣。在活动过程中，学生做出回答之后，教师可以询问学生判断的依据，引导学生分析细节。

在活动结束之后，教师可引导学生再次观察图片，发现小猫的成长规律。

参考答案：

2. 阅读理解环节。

(1) 流程图：学生根据文本信息，找出对应的关键词，填入方框内。该活动可作小组活动，学生填写完成后，教师邀请学生运用提供的句型进行展示。

(2) 阅读理解：教师引导学生根据文本信息进行阅读理解的活动。

参考答案：

(1) B (2) A (3) B (4) C (5) C

3. 写作与分享环节。

(1) 教师让学生找两张关于自己爸爸、妈妈或者两者变化的照片（一张是自己出生前父母的照片或其他旧照片，另外一张是现在的照片）。学生观察两张照片中人物的特征及变化。该活动可以布置为家庭作业，让学生和父母共同完成。

(2) 学生对比两张照片，可以观察照片上父母的外貌有什么不同或者变化，也可以询问自己的父母随着年龄的变化，在各方面能力上有什么变化。

(3) 教师引导学生考虑活动中的几个问题，思考父母的变化，并且完成日记。写作可以在课堂或者课后完成。

(4) 学生完成日记之后，自愿在小组内分享。在分享过程中，教师要求学生尽量用英语进行描述。

思维试纸:

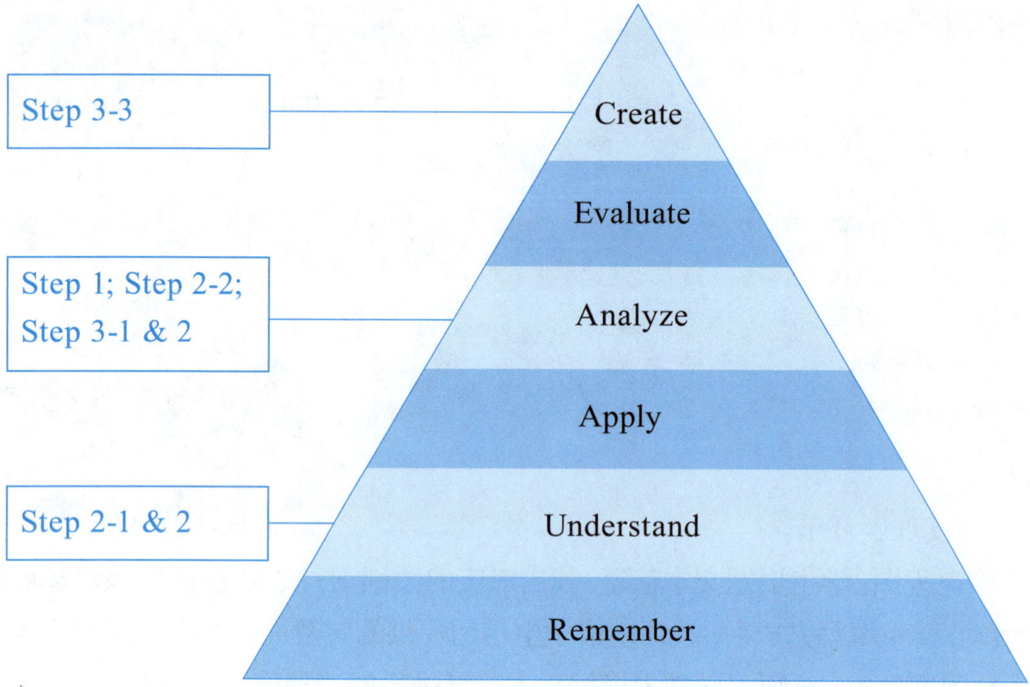

Part Three　Vocabulary

教学素材: first, second, third, fourth, fifth, twelfth, twentieth, twenty-first, twenty-third

教学步骤:

Step 1　Comprehending and Blank-filling

1. **Analyze** the form and **finish** the table.

one	first	1st
two		2nd
three	third	
four		
	fifth	
		6th

2. **Recall** and **write** the abbreviations (缩写) of the dates.

March second	January first	August third	June fifth
Mar. 2nd	________	________	________
February twelfth	**May twenty-first**	**April thirtieth**	**July fourth**
________	________	________	________

Step 2 Make Your Schedule

1. **Relate** your daily life in this month and **fill in** the month column below.

2. Let's **make** a schedule for your life. Check on your schedule. Tick if the event is completed, and cross if it is not completed.

Month:

Sunday	Monday	Tuesday	Wednesday	Thursday	Friday	Saturday

教学时长: 15 mins

教学建议:

词汇部分主要用于练习，旨在巩固词汇和语法知识。

1. Step 1 的第一个活动为自我检测。学生根据表格第一栏的数字规律完成填空。学生在课前或课后完成，教师课堂上检查。

参考答案:

second; 3rd; fourth; 4th; five; 5th; six; sixth

Step 1的第二个活动要求学生写出所给日期的缩写形式。教师可在引导学生填写一空后，再让学生进行练习，最后检查。在完成练习之后，教师也可带领学生朗读，复习月份的发音，旨在巩固月份知识。

参考答案:

Mar. 2nd; Jan. 1st; Aug. 3rd; Jun. 5th; Feb. 12th; May 21st; Apr. 30th; Jul. 4th

2. Step 2 为拓展活动，目的是让学生将日期和常识两者结合起来进行运用和巩固。教师带领学生回顾当月需要完成的任务或者比较特别的事情。学生写出该事项的关键词。学生写完事项后，进一步细化到某一天。教师带领学生先做一个示范，再让学生自行填写图表。

思维试纸:

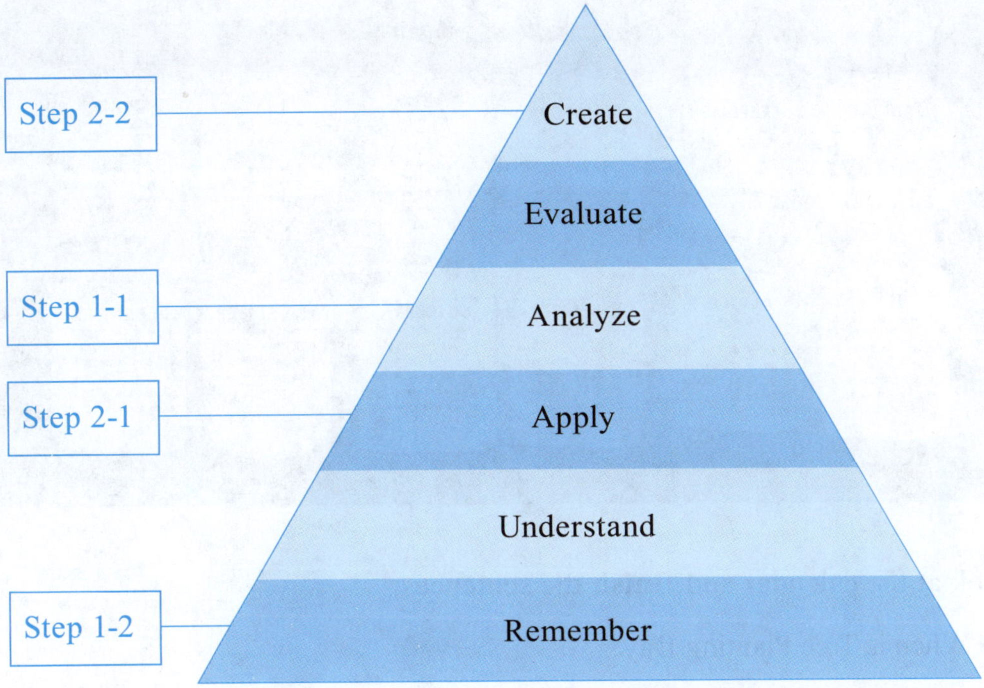

Part Four Grammar

教学素材: When is…? / It's on…

教学步骤:

Step 1 Self-checking

1. When are these special days? Please **find** and **circle** the dates on the calendar.

Tree Planting Day

Father's Day

Mother's Day

National Day

birthday

2. Look at the calendar and **finish** the sentences.

(1) — When is Tree Planting Day?

— It's ________ March 12th.

(2) — ________ ________ National Day?

— ________ ________ October ________.

(3) — ________ ________ Mother's ________?

— ________ on ________ ______.

(4) — ________ ________ ________ ________?

— ________ ________ ________ ________.

(5) — ________ ________ your birthday?

— ________ ________ ________ ________.

Step 2　Rule-finding

1. **Circle** what shares in the sentences on both sides below.

Find the Rules

When is Tree Planting Day?	It's on March 12th.
When is Mother's Day?	It's on May 10th.
When is Father's Day?	It's on June 21st.
When is National Day?	It's on October 1st.
When is your birthday?	It's on October 26th.

2. **Summarize** the sentence patterns.

The sentence patterns:

Step 3 Further Practicing

Use the words in the box to make the sentences correct.

(1) — ________ is your birthday?

— It's on September 25th.

(2) — When is Teachers' Day?

— It's ________ September 10th.

(3) — Where is she?

— She is ________ home.

(4) — ________ can you do at the party?

— I can drink some Coke.

(5) — When is your mother's birthday?

— ________ on December 27th.

A. on	B. When
C. What	D. at
E. It's	

教学时长: 15 mins

教学建议:

语法部分主要用于练习，旨在巩固词汇和语法知识。

1. 自我检测环节。

教师让学生观察图片，理解节日意思，在日历上圈出节日日期。教师邀请学生分享答案。检查完答案，学生根据日历日期填写句子。

参考答案:

(1) on (2) When is; It's on; 1st (3) When is; Day; It's; May 10th

(4) When is Father's Day; It's on June 21st (5) When is; It's on…

2. 总结规律环节。

教师引导学生观察方框中句子的共同点，然后让学生进行归纳，最后进行评价总结。

参考答案:

When is…? / It's on…

3. 巩固练习环节。

学生可自行在课前或课后完成，教师批改。课堂上，教师带领学生总结句型、存在的问题及解决办法。

参考答案:

(1) B (2) A (3) D (4) C (5) E

思维试纸:

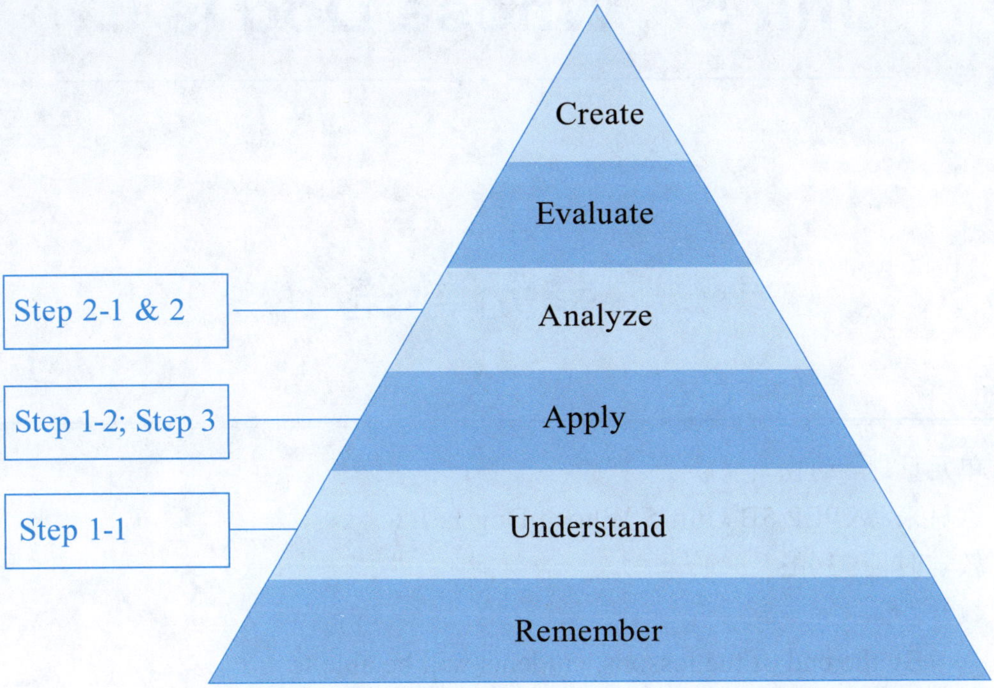
Create
Evaluate
Step 2-1 & 2
Analyze
Step 1-2; Step 3
Apply
Step 1-1
Understand
Remember

Unit 5 Whose Dog Is It?

单元导览

单元话题: 动物
素材来源: PEP 5B Unit 5 Whose Dog Is It?
教学时长: 3 hrs
教学目标:

By the end of the lessons, students will be able to

语言目标:

1. **understand** the conversations in the textbook;

2. **comprehend** the meaning of the story, **analyze** the main content, and **write** about their findings in the zoo;

3. **understand** and **remember** the meaning of the words (climbing, drinking, eating, playing, jumping and sleeping);

4. **understand** and **apply** adjective possessive pronouns and nominal possessive pronouns (his dog—his; her dog—hers; their dog—theirs; our dog—ours; my dog—mine);

5. **deduce** the rules of adjective possessive pronouns and nominal possessive pronouns;

6. **understand** the meaning of the sentence patterns (What is / are… doing? / … is / are…), **analyze** the usage of the sentence patterns, and **apply** the sentence patterns to writing and speaking.

非语言目标:

1. strengthen their analyzing skills by **analyzing** the words the owners say and the features of the dog;

2. cultivate their divergent thinking by giving open questions;

3. make decisions in different situations;

4. cultivate their awareness of protecting animals by **creating** the ways to help them;

5. work in groups to finish tasks and learn from others.

融思设计

Part One Listening and Speaking

教学素材: Part B Let's Talk

教学步骤:

Step 1 Brainstorm

Based on your experience and knowledge, fill in the bubble map to **brainstorm** common dogs' behaviors in the daily life.

Step 2 Listening Comprehension

Tick the right answer for each question.

(1) What is the name of the dog?

A. Fido. B. Fado.

(2) Whose dog is it?

A. Sam's. B. Chen Jie's.

(3) Where is the dog now?

A. In the kitchen. B. In the park.

(4) What is the dog doing?

A. Drinking water. B. Eating.

Step 3 Preparation before Speaking

1. Imagine you have a lovely dog. What is it like? Take out a piece of paper and **draw** a picture of your dog. Here are some examples for you.

You should consider:

What is it like?

Where is it?

What is it doing?

2. Please **describe** your dog. Look and finish the sentences.

(1) What is it like?

It is ____________.

Appearance (外表): big, small, tall, long, short, strong…

Color: black, white, brown, yellow, gray…

Other: cute, lovely, naughty (调皮的)…

(2) Where is it?

It is ____________.

in the park, at home, on the street (在街上)…

(3) What is it doing?

It is ____________.

running, walking, jumping, eating, drinking, sleeping, climbing…

Step 4 Speaking and Sharing

1. Share your description to your group members. After listening and sharing, each group **chooses** one picture and gives it to the host. (The host needs to stick all the pictures on the blackboard.)

2. Now go to the Lost and Found (失物招领处). Each group chooses one reporter to **retell** the description.

This is ___________'s dog.
It is…

3. After each group has described the picture, the host points at the pictures one by one, and interviews other students: Whose dog is it? Other students listen and **find** each dog's owner. (If the answer is right, he / she can get a medal (勋章) for helping.)

教学时长: 1.5 hrs

教学建议:

1. 头脑风暴环节。

该活动旨在调取学生对小狗的认知，从小狗最平常的动作入手，通过让学生填写气泡图的形式，唤起学生的旧知并训练学生的发散性思维。

2. 听力理解环节。

学生听第一遍录音后选择正确的答案，听第二遍录音时进行检查。教师可根据学生的程度确定是否再放一遍进行巩固和加深学生印象。

参考答案:

(1) A (2) B (3) A (4) B

3. 表达准备环节。

(1) 在课堂上，教师引导学生想象如果自己有一只小狗，它会长什么样子。然后，教师引导学生画出自己想象中的小狗，并要求学生考虑三个方面(小狗长什么样子，它在哪里，它在干什么)。

(2) 学生根据自己所画的小狗填写句子，旁边提示的单词供学生参考。

4. 表达与分享环节。

(1) 学生四人一组，每个组员朗读自己对小狗的描述并分享自己的图片。四人依次进行分享。

(2) 小组分享结束后，教师选出一名主持人(host)。教师引导学生在组内评价并选出一幅画给主持人。主持人需要将所有的画贴在黑板上。

(3) 小组内再选出一名同学进行全班展示。主持人依次邀请展示的同学描述自己小组的画，其他同学认真聆听。描述结束后，主持人指着黑板上的画依次问全班同学: Whose dog is it? 其他同学根据所听到的内容找出所有图画中小狗的主人。每个找对的同学可以得到一枚助人为乐勋章。

思维试纸:

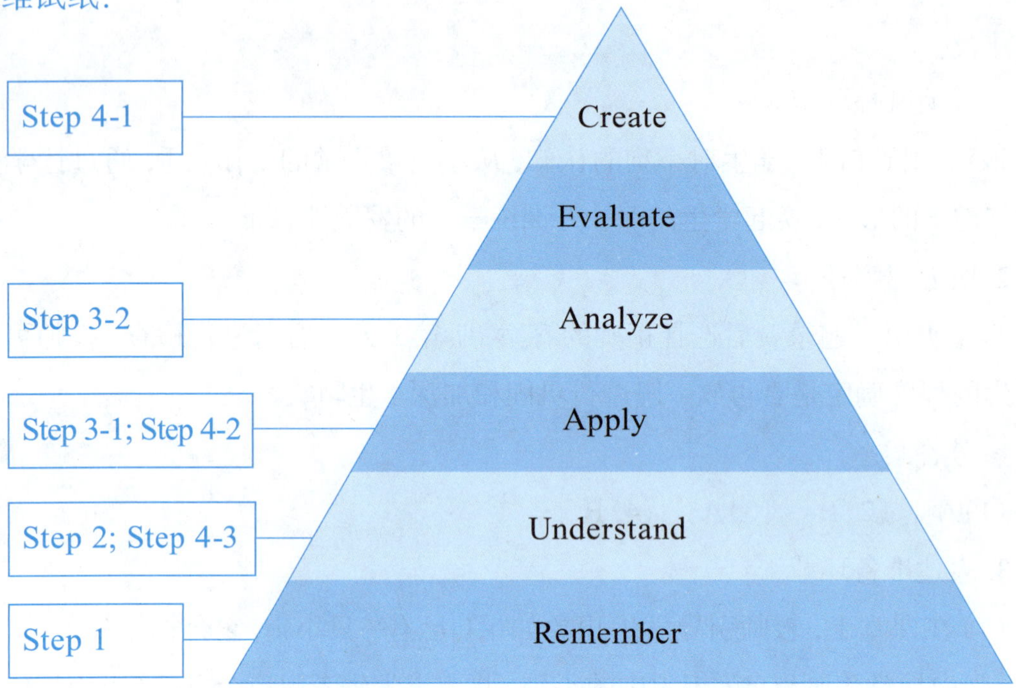

Part Two Reading and Writing

教学素材: Part B Read and Write
教学步骤:

Step 1 Preparation before Reading

1. Have you ever been to a zoo? **Recall** what you saw in the zoo. Please share with your deskmates.

2. Today Robin and Sarah want to guide you to experience being an animal keeper. Let's take a look.

(1) In the morning, Sarah needs to feed the animals. What animals are in the zoo? Look at the picture in the textbook and **circle** their names in the box.

monkeys pigs snakes sheep giraffes
lions fishes birds
tigers bears rabbits elephants horses

(2) Sarah doesn't know what they eat in the zoo. Can you help her? Please **classify** the animals according to the food, and share with us.

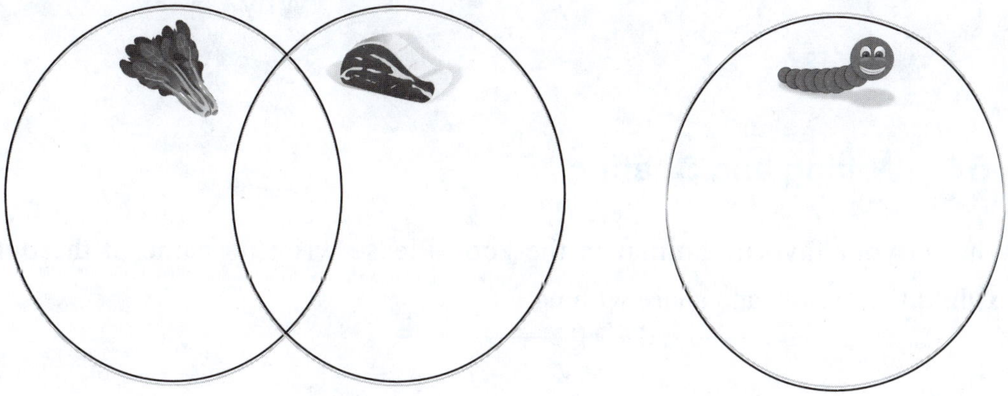

Step 2 Reading Comprehension

1. After feeding, Robin needs to make sure the animals are OK. Let's find out what they are doing. **Match** and finish this table.

What animals do you see?	What are they doing?

walking

swimming

flying

climbing

dancing

running

eating

2. **Guess** why Robin doesn't want to swim like a fish. Write down the key words.

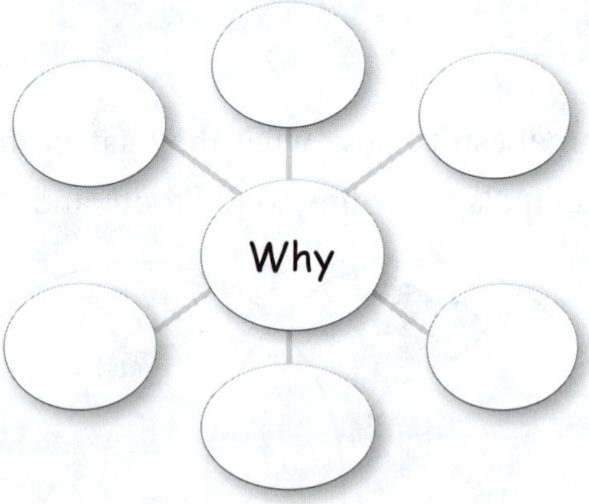

Step 3 Writing and Sharing

1. What is your favorite animal in the zoo? Please write its name in the blanks, **explain** the reason, and share with us.

My favorite animal is ____________________.

Because ______________________________.

2. What does your favorite animal look like? Please **describe** the features and **fill in** the table and share with us.

Feature	Description
eyes	
nose	
tail	
body	
color	
…	

3. At the end of the experience, **complete** your animal observation report.

Your findings should include:

(1) What animals do you see and what are they doing?

(2) Which animal is your favorite, and what does it eat and look like?

My Observation (我的观察记录)

Name: **Time:**

(1) Animals:

____

____

____

____

(2) Findings:

____

____

____

____

____

教学时长: 1 hr

教学建议:

整个阅读与写作的部分是根据Robin和Sarah一天的饲养员实践活动的顺序进行安排的,其顺序是识别动物、给动物喂食、观察动物、选择自己最喜爱的动物,最后形成一天的动物观察报告。

1. 读前准备环节。

(1) 教师引导学生调取自身储备的有关动物园动物的知识,回忆动物园里有哪些动物。

(2) 教师引导学生观察图片,并在方框内圈出相关动物的名字。

教师引导学生根据动物饮食习惯的不同,对图中的动物进行分类。最后一个框内填写特殊的食物。学生需要画出特殊的食物(如果不能够使用英文),再进一步分类。

参考答案:

(1) monkeys, tigers, bears, birds, fishes, rabbits, elephants

(2) vegetables: rabbits, elephants

meat: tigers

vegetables & meat: monkeys, bears

bugs: birds, fishes

2. 阅读理解环节。

(1) 学生回答问题,并根据短文内容填空。

参考答案:

a bear, dancing; two rabbits, eating; a tiger, running; an elephant, walking; a monkey, climbing; a bird, flying; some fishes, swimming

(2) 教师引导学生想象Robin不想像鱼一样游泳的原因,并鼓励学生尽量用英语回答,用中文作答亦可。

3. 写作与分享环节。

(1) 根据学生的观察,教师让学生选择自己最喜爱的动物并解释原因。

(2) 教师引导学生观察所选择的动物,描述其特征。表格最后一行的填写内容留给学生自主思考,是否还有其他特征并进行描述。

（3）在写作时，“Animals”后要求填写所观察到的动物。“Findings”中分为两个部分：一是要求学生将活动2观察到的内容运用“I can see ___. It is ____.”的句型进行描述；二是学生需要运用 “It has…” “It is…” “It likes…”等句型描述自己最喜爱的动物。

思维试纸:

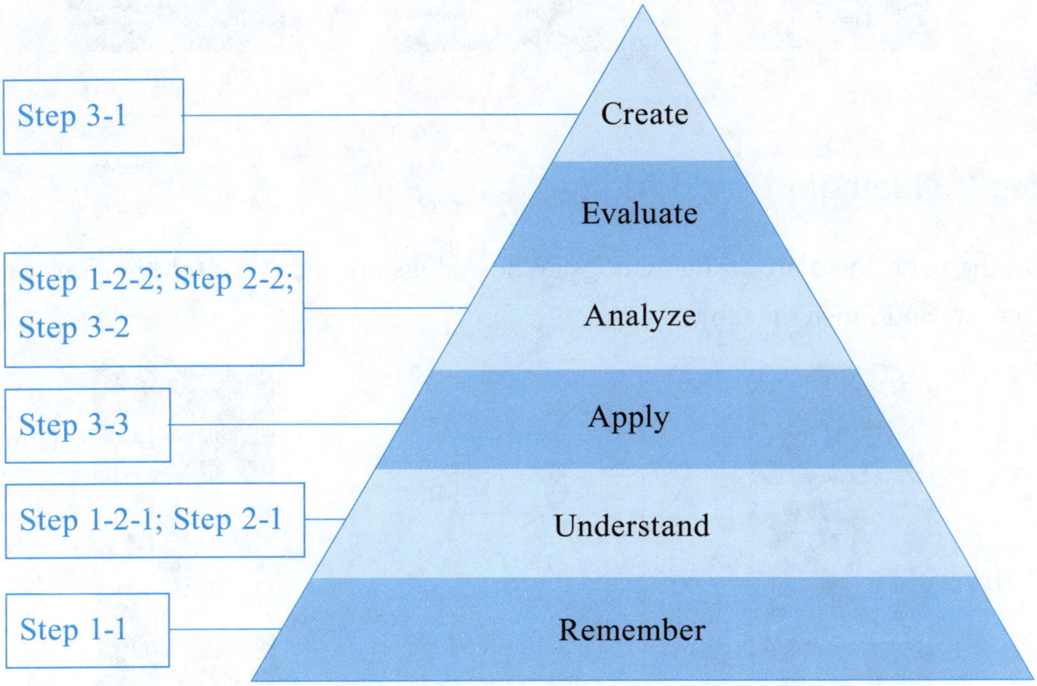

Part Three Vocabulary

教学素材: mine, yours, his, hers, theirs, ours, climbing, eating, playing, jumping, drinking, sleeping

教学步骤:

Step 1 Recalling

Look at the dogs. What are they doing? **Recall** and write the words under the pictures.

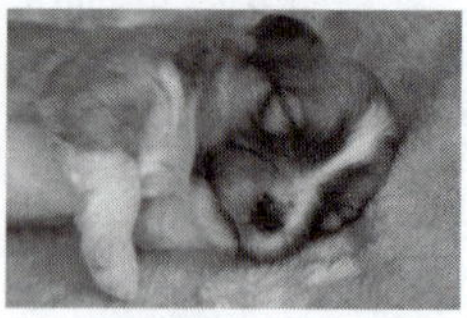

Step 2　Matching and Writing

1. In the park, there are so many dogs. Whose dogs are they? **Match** the dogs to the owners and finish the table.

Owner	Dog
Hank	
Pam	
Helen	
Ben	
Tim and Tom	

2. **Read** the above table, and **use** the words below to complete all the sentences.

my your his her our your their

mine yours his hers ours yours theirs

Dog A is Helen's dog. It is her dog. It is hers.
Dog B is ________ dog. It is ________ dog. It is ________.
Dog F is ________ dog. It is ________ dog. It is ________.
Dog G is ________ dog. It is ________ dog. It is ________.
Dogs C, D and E are ________ dogs. They are ________ dogs.
They are ________.

教学时长: 15 mins

教学建议:

词汇部分主要用于练习,旨在巩固词汇和语法知识。

1. 学生看图填词:学生观察图片,填写描述小狗动作的单词。学生可自行在课前或课后完成,教师课堂上检查。

参考答案:

(1) running　(2) sleeping　(3) drinking

(4) playing　(5) eating　(6) climbing

2. 匹配与书写练习。

(1) 根据图中各条线,学生进行匹配,并且填写表格。

(2) 根据形容词物主代词和名词性物主代词对照关系,学生进行填空练习,教师可在引导学生填写一题之后,让学生自行练习,最后检查。

Ben's, his, his

Hank's, his, his

Tim and Tom's, their, theirs

Pam's, her, hers

思维试纸:

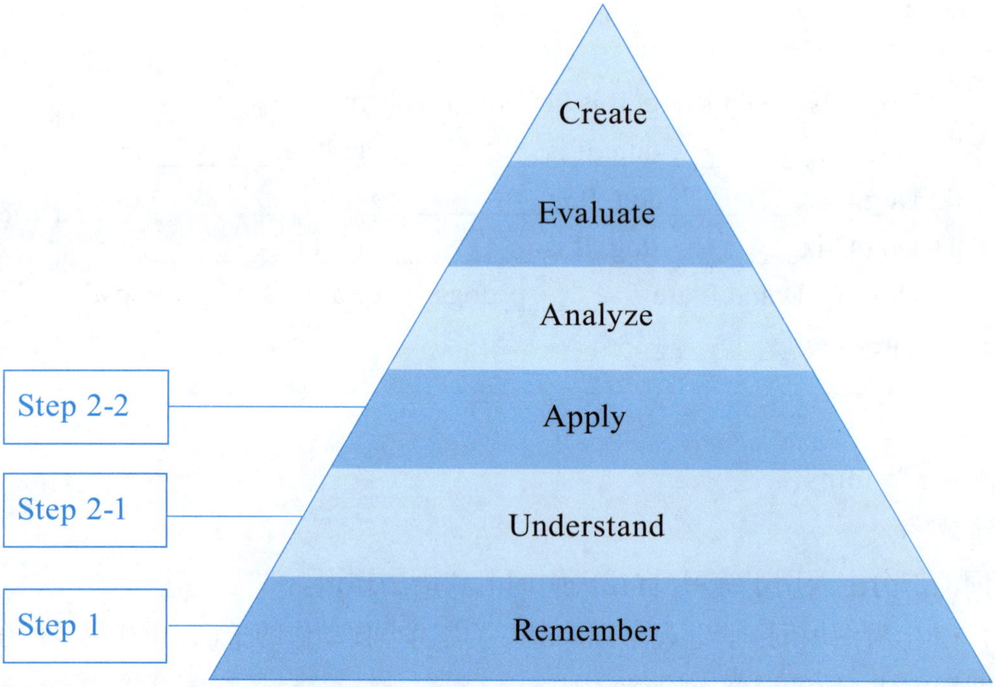

Part Four Grammar

教学素材: What is / are... doing? / ... is / are...

教学步骤:

Step 1 Finding Differences

1. Look at the two pictures. Can you **find** 3 differences? Please circle them out and share with us.

Find 3 Differences

Picture A

Picture B

2. **Fill in** the blanks according to the above pictures.

(1) — What is Giraffe D doing?

— Giraffe D ________ ____________.

(2) — What ________ the dogs ____________?

— The dogs ________ ____________.

(3) — __________ ______ Monkey H __________?

— __________ ________ ______________.

(4) — ________ is ________ ____________?

— ________ ________ eating.

Step 2 Rule-finding

1. **Circle** what shares in the sentences on both sides below.

Find the Rules

What is the pig doing?	The pig is sleeping.
What is the giraffe doing?	The giraffe is drinking.
What are the dogs doing?	The dogs are running.
What are the rabbits doing?	The rabbits are jumping.

2. **Summarize** the sentence patterns.

The sentence patterns:

Step 3 Further Practicing

Look at the picture and choose 3 animals to test your partners. You can **use** the above sentence patterns.

(1) —____________________?

—____________________.

(2) —____________________?

—____________________.

(3) —____________________?

—____________________.

教学时长: 15 mins

教学建议:

语法部分主要用于练习, 旨在巩固词汇和语法知识。学生可自行在课前或课后完成, 教师批改。课堂上, 教师带领学生总结句型、存在的问题及解决办法。

1. 教师带领学生完成找不同的活动。在找不同时, 教师主要引导学生发现动物动作的不同。在学生进行分享时, 教师引导学生尽量使用句型: Monkey G in Picture A is eating. Monkey H in Picture B is climbing.

教师引导学生根据发现的不同进行填写练习, 然后检查。

参考答案:

(1) is, drinking　(2) are, doing, are, running

(3) What, is, doing, Monkey H, is, climbing

(4) What, Monkey G, doing, Monkey G, is

2. 教师先让学生观察句子, 然后总结句型。

参考答案:

The sentence patterns: "What is / are... doing?" "... is / are..."

3. 教师让学生观察图片, 应用所总结出的句型互相出题, 巩固对句型的掌握。

思维试纸:

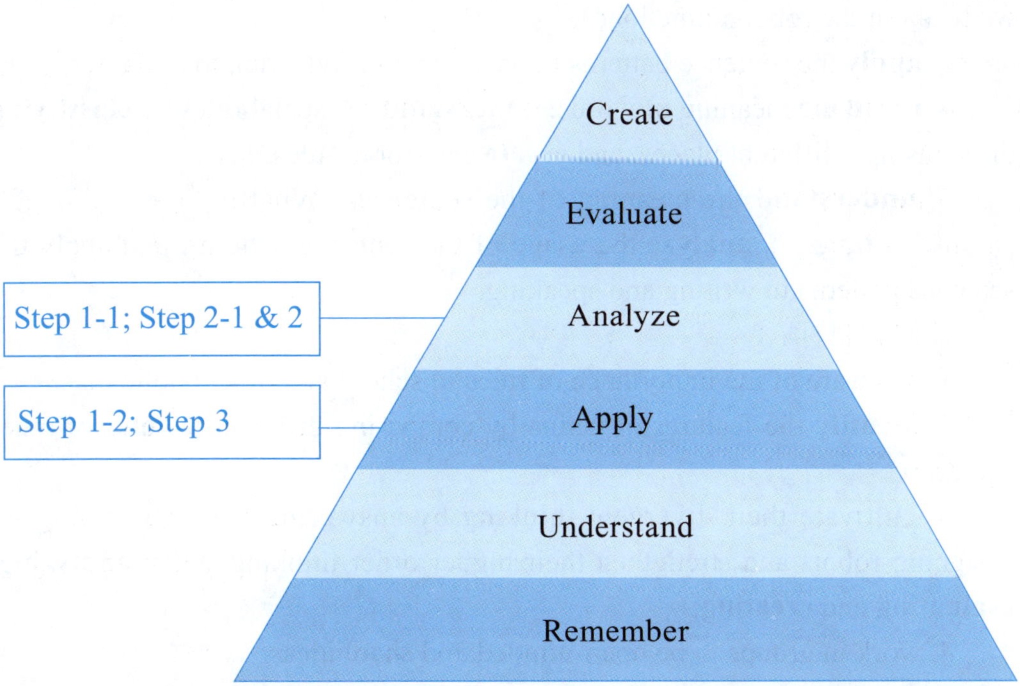

Unit 6 Work Quietly!

单元导览

单元话题: 公共规章
素材来源: PEP 5B Unit 6 Work Quietly!
教学时长: 3 hrs
教学目标:

By the end of the lessons, students will be able to

语言目标:

1. **understand** the conversations in the textbook and describe the photos by **applying** the sentence patterns: What is he doing? / He is…

2. **comprehend** the meaning of the story, **analyze** the main content and **write** about the robot's function;

3. **apply** the sentence patterns to writing an introduction to a robot;

4. **recall** the meaning of words, **understand** the social rules by **classifying** the signs into different places, and **create** classroom rules;

5. **understand** the meaning of the sentences (What is / are… doing? / … am / is / are…), **analyze** the usage of the sentence patterns, and apply the sentence patterns to writing and speaking.

非语言目标:

1. be aware of the importance of rules in school and other public places;

2. **identify** the features of China by comparing different features of other countries;

3. cultivate their divergent thinking by answering open questions and designing robots and strengthen their higher order thinking skills: **analyzing**, **evaluating** and **creating**;

4. work in groups to be open-minded and share ideas.

融思设计

Part One Listening and Speaking

教学素材: Part B Let's Talk

教学步骤:

Step 1 Listening Comprehension

1. Look at the picture and **select** where Tom is.

   A. In the classroom.

   B. On the playground.

   C. In the library.

2. Tom sees a boy. Let's listen to the conversation between them and **find out** what the boy's name is.

His name is ___________.

3. Listen and **tick**. What should Tom pay attention to?

A. 

B. 

C. 

Step 2 Preparation before Speaking

1. At the beginning of the school, the students came to the classroom. Look at this classroom. What can you see? Please **identify** and share with your friends.

I can see ______________.

2. Do you like this classroom? Why? Please **judge** and **write** your reasons.

I _________ (like / don't like) this classroom.
Reason 1:
Reason 2:
…

3. Should we make rules for the classroom? Please **judge**, **write** your reasons and share with your group members.

I think we ________ (should / shouldn't) make rules for the classroom.
Because…

4. If you are the monitor of this class, please think about what rules you can make. **Use** the sentence patterns and share with us.

Rule 1:
Rule 2:
Rule 3:
Rule 4:
…

Sentence patterns:
No + doing (e.g. No eating!)
Keep + *adj*. (e.g. Keep clean.)
Do + *adv*. (e.g. Talk quietly.)

Step 3 Speaking and Sharing

The principal (校长) gives you a task. You need to **introduce** the school to the first-grade students to help them understand the rules better.

library

dining hall

computer room

playground

1. One group chooses one place. Think and **write** the key words of the place.

   You should consider:

   Where is it?

   What can they do?

   What cannot they do?

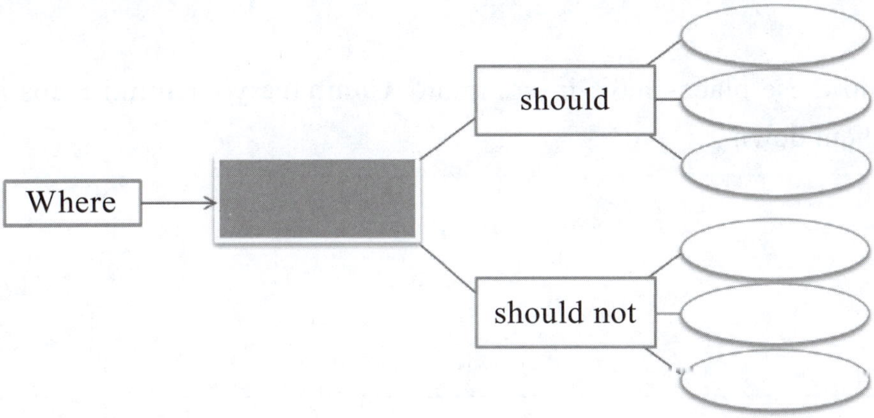

   You can add more.

2. Each group presents the mind map in class, and other group members will be the principals to **evaluate** the proposals (提案) and **explain** the reasons. After the presentation, each group needs to **amend** (修改) the proposals.

> I think it is good / bad. Because…
> (If it's bad) They should change (the bad one) to…

3. Let's regroup and **introduce** your place to the new group members. Other students need to **draw** at least 2 mind maps while listening.

Hi, I am your guide. I will introduce this place to you. Here is ______.
Here are some rules: One…; Two…
You can… here.

4. What do these places have in common? **Compare** your mind maps and then write them down.

教学时长: 1.5 hrs

教学建议:

1. 听力理解环节。

教师播放两遍录音。第一遍播放录音后，学生确定图片中的地点和人物名字，第二遍播放录音后，学生确定在图书馆汤姆需要注意哪些事项。教师可根据学生的程度决定是否放第三遍进行巩固和加深学生印象。

参考答案:

(1) C (2) John (3) A; C

2. 表达准备环节。

教师引导学生观察图片，让学生归纳在图片中能看到的内容，教师需要特别引导学生观察教室中不文明的行为，然后询问学生是否喜欢这个教室，并引导学生阐明理由。

教师引导学生了解设置规则的重要性，并举例说明，再让学生分享理由。

教师引导学生制定班规。教师引导学生考虑班规应包含哪些方面。学生可利用所提供的句型，进行表达和分析。

3. 表达与分享环节。

场所从教室扩展到学校的其他地方，假设学生作为志愿者，为一年级新生介绍学校。每个小组负责介绍一个地方，需要考虑这是哪里，有些什么规则，学生日常能在这里做什么。

第一步：首先在小组内，学生需要完成一个如何介绍所选定地点的思维图。第二步：小组进行班级展示，其他小组需要观察，评价他们的提案是好是坏，并且给出理由，不好的话应该怎样修改。第三步：重新分小组，保证新小组内小组成员介绍不同的地方，每个同学在听的时候需要完成除了自己小组之外的其他思维图(至少两个)，可以仿照提供的示范图，也可重新创作。第四步：教师让学生对所画思维图进行比较，思考这些地方有没有规则是通用的，或者有没有什么事情是在这些地方都能做的。

思维试纸：

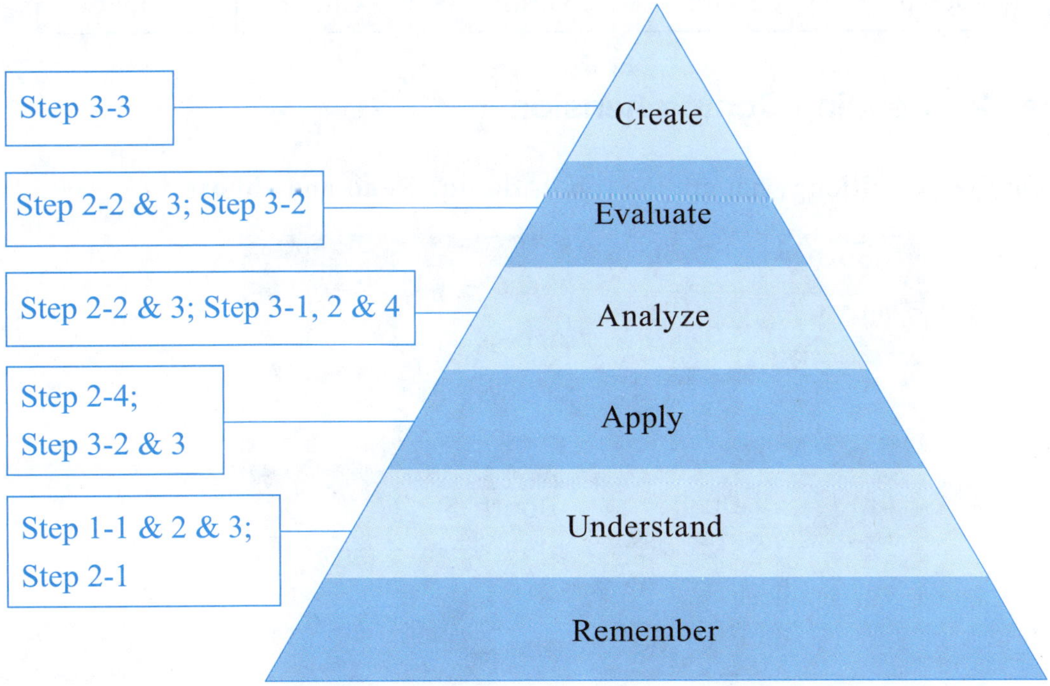

Part Two Reading and Writing

教学素材: Part B Read and Write

教学步骤:

Step 1 Preparation before Reading

Today there is a world robot exhibition. Robots come from many countries. Can you send each robot to the corresponding country's booth? **Match** robots to the countries.

Japan	Spain	U.S.A.	China	Canada

Step 2 Reading Comprehension

1. On the exhibition, what are the robots doing? **Read** and **choose**.

(1) The Canadian robot is __________.

(2) Asako is __________.

(3) The Spanish robot is __________.

(4) The Chinese robot is __________.

(5) Robin is __________.

drawing pictures
singing
making sushi
eating sushi
listening to music
playing music
doing kung fu
doing exercise

2. What can the robot do? **Brainstorm** and **explain** the reasons.

He can ________________, because __________.

Step 3 Writing and Sharing

1. In the next year, we still have the world robot exhibition. Can you design a robot which shows the Chinese features? What are Chinese features besides kung fu? **Brainstorm** your ideas.

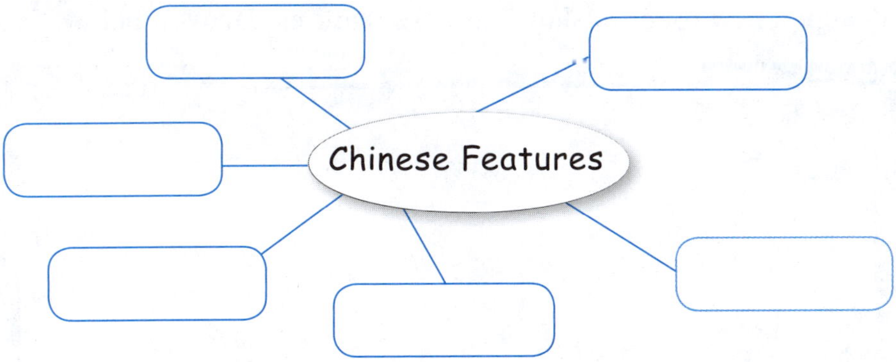

2. How will your robot show these features?
Think about the following questions and list your ideas.

(1) What action is the robot doing? **Read** the pictures and **write** your choice in the box.

play　listen　eat　do kung fu　drink　sing　dance　draw pictures

The robot is ______________________________.

(2) **Choose** what dress the robot wears.

Hanfu (汉服)

Qipao (旗袍)

Chinese tunic suit (中山装)

…

(3) **Choose** what the robot holds in hand.

fan (扇子)

sword (剑)

flute (笛子)

…

3. Let's **design** a new robot to show Chinese features. **Draw** it below.

Robot Introduction

Name: ______ Color: ______ Size: ______

In the picture: ______________________________

____

____

My robot can also: ______________________________

____

____

4. Introduce your robot to your group members. Let's **choose** the robot that best fits the Chinese features. And **summarize** the reasons below.

We think ______'s robot is the best.

The reasons are:

(1) ______________________________

____

(2) ______________________________

____

(3) ______________________________

____

教学时长: 1 hr

教学建议:

1. 读前准备环节。

教师引导学生通过观察，将机器人与国家进行匹配，激发学生的学习兴趣。在活动过程中，学生做出回答之后，教师可以询问学生匹配的依据。

2. 阅读理解环节。

（1）回答问题：学生根据短文内容选择并填写答案，教师引导学生运用句型“The robot is...”描述动作。

参考答案：

（1）drawing pictures　（2）making sushi　（3）playing music

（4）doing kung fu　（5）listening to music

（2）头脑风暴：教师引导学生根据读前活动中的线索思考美国机器人能做什么、为什么，并鼓励学生尽量用英语回答，用中文作答亦可。

3. 写作与分享环节。

（1）教师引导学生思考：体现中国特色的东西有哪些，例如大熊猫、瓷器以及各类传统文化等。思考之后，学生在气泡图内进行记录，可用中文记录。

（2）学生根据活动1填写的与中国特色相关的事物，进行绘画创作。

教师需要引导学生一步思考：机器人在干什么，穿什么服装，手里拿着什么。在每个步骤教师都需要为学生准备相关词汇示例。学生也可以自行补充。教师可以提前布置任务，让学生小组分工在家搜集资料，进而根据所选内容创作机器人的绘画，然后根据所画内容描述机器人的名字、颜色、大小以及功能等信息。

（3）学生将自己的机器人介绍给其他组内成员，小组选出最符合中国特色的机器人，并且记录下原因。注意在分享过程中，教师要求学生尽量用英语进行描述。

思维试纸：

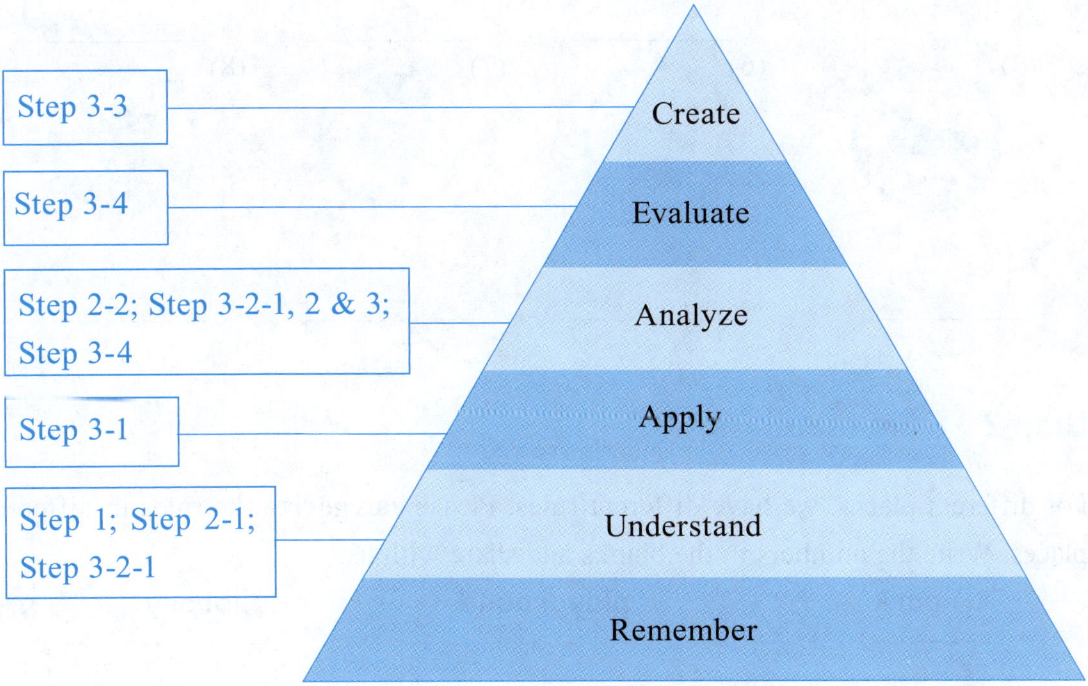

Part Three　Vocabulary

教学素材：keep to the right, keep your desk clean, talk quietly

教学步骤：

Step 1　Understanding and Blank-filling

Did you see these signs in real life? What do they mean? Please **match** and write.

Talk quietly.	Keep to the right.	Keep your desk clean.
No touching!	No feeding!	No eating!
No climbing!	No smoking!	

(1)  ________

(2)  ________

(3)  ________

(4)  ________

(5)  ________

(6)  ________

(7)  ________

(8)  ________

Step 2 Rule-matching

For different places, we have different rules. Please **categorize** the rules in different places. Write the numbers in the blanks and share with us.

park

playground

library

zoo

restaurant

Step 3 Rule-making

In our classroom, do we have rules? Let's **make** rules for our class. Please **draw** the sign and write the meaning.

______________ ______________

Sentence patterns:
No + doing (e.g. No eating!)
Keep + *adj*. (e.g. Keep clean.)
Do + *adv*. (e.g. Talk quietly.)

____

教学时长: 15 mins

教学建议:

词汇部分旨在巩固词汇和语法知识。

1. 学生观察图标，猜测标志的含义，根据标志的含义进行图文匹配练习。学生自行在课前或课后完成，教师课堂上检查。

参考答案:

(1) Talk quietly.

(2) Keep to the right.

(3) Keep your desk clean.

(4) No eating!

(5) No smoking!

(6) No touching!

(7) No feeding!

(8) No climbing!

2. 学生根据Step 1所填写的标志含义进行分类。教师可告诉学生同一规则可用于多个场所。分类结束后，学生进行分享，其他同学表明是否同意。

3. 教师让学生回想教室里是否有任何规则，如果有，就将规则显性化，做成标志或标语张贴在教室内。如果没有，教师就引导学生在小组内思考并创作标志或标语，并和大家分享这样做的目的。

思维试纸:

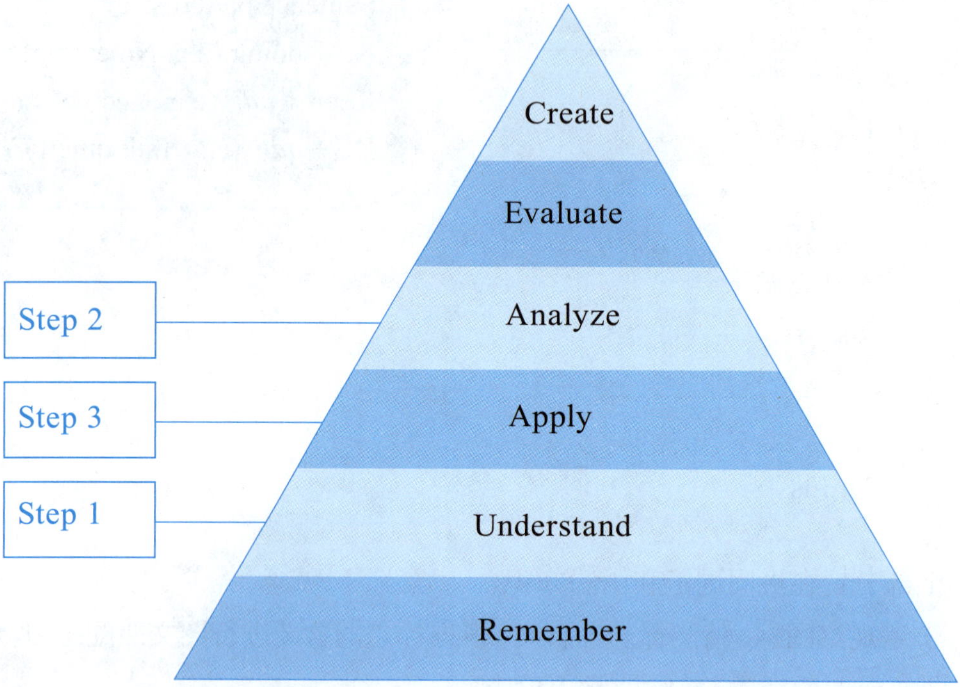

Part Four　Grammar

教学素材: The "be" form agrees with its subject in person.
教学步骤:

Step 1　Comprehending and Blank-filling

What are the children doing in the photo? Discuss and **fill in** the blanks.

This is my photo.

(1) This is me. I ________ ______________.

(2) These are ________ and ________. They ________ fighting.

(3) This is Lily. She ________ ________.

(4) This is Mike. He ________ ________.

(5) This is Tom. ________ ________ ______________.

Step 2 Rule-finding

1. **Circle** what shares in the sentences on both sides.

Find the Rules

What are you doing?	I am running.
What is she doing?	She is sleeping.
What is he doing?	He is drawing.
What is it doing?	It is drinking water.
What are you doing?	We are playing.
What are they doing?	They are having English class.

2. **Summarize** the sentence patterns.

The sentence patterns:

Step 3 Further Practicing

1. **Classify** the words and put them in the right boxes.

they　you　it　I　she　he　we

(1)　(2)　(3)

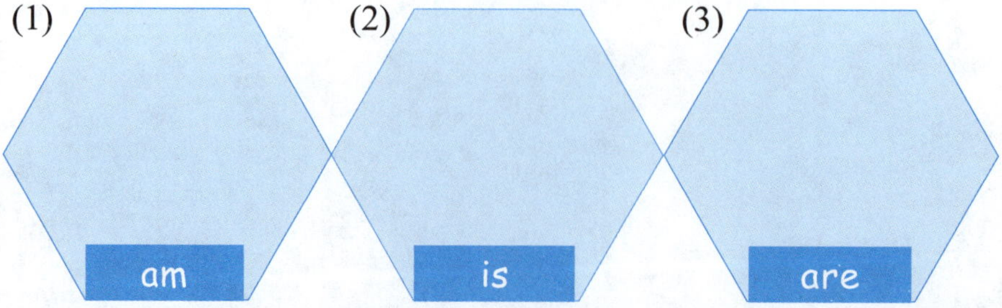

2. If you are an English teacher, you need to **find** and **correct** the mistakes in the following exercises. Can you find them?

(C) (1) — What are you doing?

— I _____ running.

A. am B. is C. are

(C) (2) — What is she doing?

— She _____ sleeping.

A. are B. does C. is

(B) (3) — What _____ you doing?

— We are playing.

A. am B. is C. are

(A) (4) The children _____ football.

A. is playing B. are playing C. am playing

(C) (5) Listen! She _____ in the classroom.

A. is singing B. is sing C. to sing

(C) (6) Jack and Kitty _____ in the pool. Let's join them.

A. is swimming B. am swimming C. are swimming

教学时长：15 mins

教学建议：

语法部分主要用于练习，旨在巩固词汇和语法知识。学生可自行在课前或课后完成，教师批改。课堂上，教师带领学生总结句型、存在的问题及解决办法。

1. 教师带领学生观察图片，可以询问学生图片上的人物在做什么。经过口头表达之后，教师带领学生完成填空练习。

参考答案：

(1) am; swimming　　(2) Tim; Andy, are

(3) is; jumping　　(4) is; eating　　(5) He; is; running

2. 教师带领学生观察句子，让学生总结句型，培养学生的自主学习能力。

3. 教师可布置学生课后完成，让学生体验当老师，让他们进行试卷的批改练习。

参考答案：

Step 3-1:

(1) I　　(2) she; he; it　　(3) you; they; we

Step 3-2:

(1) A　(2) C　(3) C　(4) B　(5) A　(6) C

思维试纸：

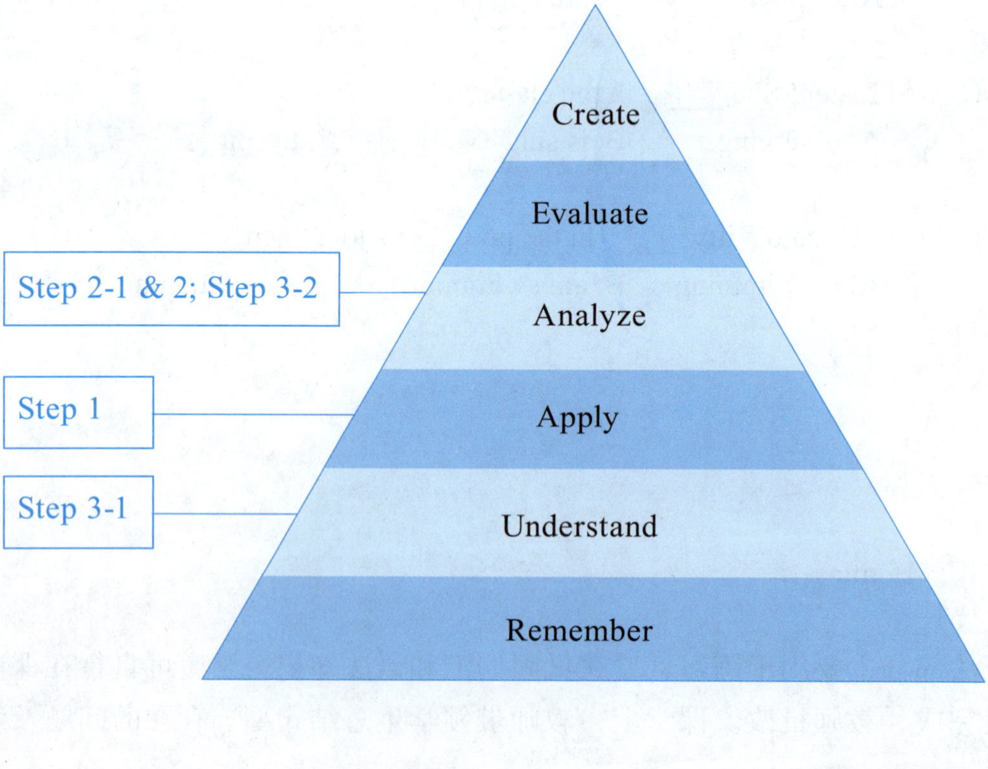